CONCENTRATION

AND THE

ACQUIREMENT

OF

PERSONAL MAGNETISM

(1910)

Contents: Thought and the Brain; The Will; Magnetic Power; Concentration; Personal Magnetism; Breathing and Physical Exercises; The Magnetic Gaze; Diet; Magnetic Healing.

Hashnu O. Hara

ISBN 1-56459-881-0

CONTENTS

—:o:—

INTRODUCTION

—:o:—

IN giving this series of lessons to the public at a nominal fee, I believe I am really doing something which will be of great benefit to all who need a helmsman to guide the rudder of the good boat "Thought" to the harbour of Success.

Thought, *unorganised*, is so much waste matter; Thought, ORGANISED, is the greatest power in the world, greater even than the almighty Dollar, for it *commands* filthy lucre and bids grim poverty farewell —for ever! It commands *love*, which filthy *lucre* can't, and it commands all that makes life worth living.

That it is necessary to undergo special mental training to produce this state of mental organisation is very apparent, and that people desire daily more light, more knowledge, and for means to overcome their state of ignorance is, as sure as "eggs are eggs," the reason why Personal Magnetism and the consideration of the Thought Forces have become such a cult.

Personal Magnetism means ***health***, ***happiness***, ***Power*** and ***Success***.

Those who want these things and all they stand for, follow the rules I give you in these pages; read, mark, learn and inwardly digest each lesson, and if you do not live to bless the wonderful force known as Personal or Animal Magnetism; if you do not realise within yourself a new found happiness, ***because*** you realise that you are not the weak, downtrodden creature you have so long considered yourself, but a glorified, radiant, happy being; then, I say, my name is not

O HASHNU HARA.

Concentration and the Acquirement of Personal Magnetism

LESSON I

THAT a course of lessons fully illustrating the action of thought, explaining its composition, and the correct method of using it, would prove a boon to many students of the Occult and mental sciences, who find this a very great drawback to serious advancement, appears almost a certainty.

The methods usually advocated seem to me very impractical; in the first place, how can a man who has never learnt to control thought in every-day matters, such as banishing business worries when he comes home, or goes to bed, or in learning to control small habits, suddenly sit down and "*concentrate on Spirit,*" when probably his very idea of spirit is such as to awaken all his dormant fancies, and to call forth not one image, but hundreds? Then he fondly believes he is concentrating, until the utter absence of results proves that he has done no such thing, and he begins all over again.

It is only what may be expected, and even a general attempt to simplify the matter would be welcome; but I have had so many letters and so many appeals from men and women who cannot master this one subject—quite the most important in the whole school of Metaphysical and Occult teachings—the door, in fact, which will open to them the whole vista held out in books, an entrancing vision of knowledge, of health, of happiness, and the unseen, which too often will remain in books, simply because the initial step is too difficult—that I have made a great effort to meet the demand in a popular and practical form.

First of all I will beg of my pupils to begin at the bottom. Do not try to concentrate your thoughts on spirit before you are quite sure—

First. As to what THOUGHT is composed of.

Second. That you are able to concentrate your mind on some unimportant mundane matter, to the exclusion of all else.

Third. Do not try to concentrate your mind for half an hour at a time, until you can concentrate for two consecutive minutes.

Fourth. What spirit is.

I advise the student to practise keeping his mind on one subject for a minute at a time, and then gradually increase the time from day to day.

If you intended to train for, say, a foot race, you would not start with a twenty-mile walk after having been out of training for a long time. Nor if a little child is being taught how to read is he given a difficult scientific book to begin with. Yet men and women are put to a task far more difficult than these, without any preparation or gradual initiation into the processes employed.

Take some subject you are very much interested in for the commencement, then for one minute hold this before your mind's eye, try to see it in your imagination, and if you fail, wait another hour or so and then try again.

By these means you gradually increase the elasticity of your brain, which, by continual exercises, can be expanded and made to perform tasks which were originally impossible. The next thing is to consider the part our brain plays in the matter of thought generation.

Look upon the brain simply as a very delicate machine, a dynamo which generates thought as an ordinary dynamo generates electricity. The construction of this machine needs some consideration, for it is known that certain parts of the brain are put to certain uses, and that a brain left dormant grows gradually incapable of anything much above involuntary action, and that if certain parts even of the brain are neglected they in turn become atrophied and are useless.

The accompanying diagram shows the relative parts of the brain, and the work they do is as follows:—

Fig. 1 is the cerebrum, and consists of two hemispheres, which are separated by a very deep fissure. The cerebrum is composed of a thick layer of grey matter, surrounding white fibrous nerve substance. The grey matter is drawn up into folds, or convolutions, and the whole is covered by a delicate membrane composed of arteries and veins, supported by tissue.

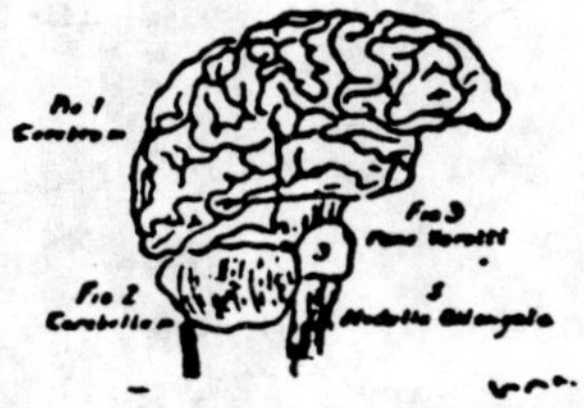

This part of the brain is the seat of sensation, of will, of intelligence, and also of the emotions; if this part of the brain is injured, the power of manifesting mental faculties is more or less lost.

Fig. 2 is the lesser brain, or cerebellum, and this guards and regulates the involuntary muscles and movements of the mind and body. I have always placed the subconscious mind here; it seems the most reasonable locality to apportion it to, for the subconscious mind is certainly an involuntary worker;

it also depends very little upon the will or the emotions, for all the will-power in the world will not make it manifest if it is not in the state to do so, and the every-day working brain has quite enough to do to look after its own without taking on another function.

Fig. 3, the pons varolli, and Fig. 5, the medulla oblongata, do not immediately concern us, although, of course, their own work is very important. Thus, if the medulla oblongata is destroyed, death at once ensues.

From the under surface of the brain twelve pairs of nerves are given off, called the cranial nerves; each pair supply some sense to the body, generated by the brain machine, just as a dynamo turns out its streams of electricity. One pair of nerves supply the sense of smell; the next the optic nerves; the third pair move the eyeballs; the fourth supply the skin of the face, the muscles of the lower jaw, and the tongue; the sixth pair are supplied to the muscles which turn the eyeballs outwards; the seventh pair supply fibres to the muscles of the face; the eighth pair supply the ear; the ninth pair are mixed nerves and they enable us to taste, and also supply the nerves to the pharynx; the tenth pair are very important mixed nerves which send fibres to the larynx, lungs, heart, stomach and liver;

the eleventh pair are motor nerves which supply certain muscles to the neck; the twelfth pair are sending fibres to the tongue. So here we get a clear idea of our thought machine, a good thing to start with, since certainly no other kind of engineer would attempt to drive a machine of which he was absolutely ignorant. This direct arrangement from the brain centre explains to a great extent how the form of concentration called *mental healing* can affect the body, and rebuild the tissues.

For each pair of nerves will carry the message given to them by the brain, and it naturally depends upon the message as to the effect produced. Here we get the machine we have to work with, and having mastered the technical parts of it, we will now proceed to see how thought acts, and how concentration affects thought.

It has long been a matter of consideration and study to me as to where the will really is located, and in this matter of concentration it is doubly important, because without the WILL man cannot possibly concentrate. It is the master of the Thought Machine, and I have found that the best way to meet the difficulty is to look upon the WILL as the OVER SOUL, that part of man which never dies, and which is carried on from incarnation to incarnation. I am assuming the theory of reincarnation to be something more than theory. It has been given to me to remember past lives, although only two or three; but even if one can remember any it surely renders the theory a fact.

This OVER SOUL, or will-power, is the force which sets the brain in motion, and which determines what effect the thought generated will have, and also what strength; it rests within ourselves to decide the stage we are to reach in each successive incarnation (after we have been through a certain number), yet if we seek the intelligent co-operation of the over soul we can, if we so desire, accomplish in one life what might otherwise take centuries to perform.

LESSON II

THE seat of WILL, or the over soul, may, I think, be safely placed in the NERVE AURA surrounding the brain.

The exact nature of thought has not, so far as I have been able to discover, ever been fully explained. There is no doubt but that thought is of atomic origin, else I do not quite see how, in accordance with Nature's law, it could travel through the ether.

In regarding the action of thought in the ether, we are too much in danger of regarding the ether as something outside ourselves, and thought as an unconsidered and unknown quantity, a mistake which must be rigorously guarded against.

The ether permeates our whole body, and because of this wonderful invisible medium, thought, magnetism, and other known substances of a similar nature can attract to themselves matter from out the universe; thought, of course, having a greater power of attraction than any other substance. There is nothing in the world which can prevent this attraction, no matter what may intervene between the thought and the object it seeks. The reason for this may be summed up in one word—ether. This acts as a conducting medium for the light waves which travel from the most distant planets and fixed stars, light which takes ten years to reach our little earth; and it acts as a conducting medium for our thought, whether we desire to send it to the other side of the earth, or to some far distant region in the unknown, or back, back into the long forgotten past, or forward into the yet unexplored future.

I have frequently held forth respecting the nature of that invisible substance called *ether*, but for the benefit of new readers, at the risk of boring the old, I will repeat myself.

The ether, then, is an invisible medium filling all space; it is accepted by scientists as a *necessity* to account for the transmission of LIGHT through space where no ordinary medium, such as *air*, is to be found.

It is said by scientists to be of a smooth, jelly-like substance, and by Rosicrucians it is looked upon as living flame. We are at present more concerned with the scientific standpoint of what is called the "luminiferous ether." As my readers can readily understand, there must be *some* substance to fill all space, or we could get no light from sun or moon, or the far distant stars.

This light *travels* through the ether by means of "*waves*," that is, the tiny atoms, or particles, travel through space in a series of concentric (that is, from a common centre) waves, each particle communicating motion to the next adjoining particle, and so on. Remember, too, that each particle, or atom, becomes, in its turn, a centre of disturbance, sending out new waves. These wave lengths are exceedingly minute, and travel at an immense speed. They follow the wave form usual to *water* when, say, a stone is thrown in to cause a disturbance. There is the crest of the wave and the trough, and although the scientific method of measuring the length of these waves does not affect us at present, measured they are.

We know that *light* travels through ether by means of *waves* continually spreading outward; that a RAY of light is really non-existent. Light travels in *minute* particles, or atoms, and THOUGHT is propelled through the ether and through *space* in a similar manner to light.

You will consider the brain as a dynamo, only, of course, more powerful than any other known machine, and more delicately constructed. Man, as a race, is in constant danger of under-estimating the power of this machine, simply because he cannot CONCEIVE of such power.

From the central point of the brain, where motion is so intense, it almost appears at a standstill, thought radiates outward, as light radiates from our central point of energy—the sun.

We have seen, first, the machine which generates thought, and secondly, the medium through which thought is propelled in its journey from one point of the globe to another.

The NATURE of thought is such that it is invisible as far as ocular demonstration is concerned, but its POWER is such that it is manifested in our daily life on every hand.

I assume thought to be of atomic origin, and, as I have already explained, the ether is a smooth, jelly-like substance with the property of transmitting atoms and molecules (a molecule is a group of two or more atoms) through space (which it entirely fills) at a terrific speed, the speed, of course, depending entirely upon the nature and size of the atom. Thought atoms are so infinitesimal that they probably exceed the highest known rate of speed, for the smaller the atom the higher and swifter the rate of vibration.

Whenever anybody thinks, even on the most trivial matter, they at once set up a stress (or disturbance) in the ether, and all around them becomes disturbed. If the thought was feeble, the disturbance will be merely local, and affect nobody, although, if charged with anger, worry, or discontent, it will affect the thinker very much for evil.

Such thoughts upset the ether, recoil upon the internal organism through the brain, and set up a state of irritation similar to the mental process, thus affecting not only the secretions of the vital organs, but surrounding the whole with a negative aura, which destroys the waves of love and good feeling which would otherwise surround that person. Then also, in a slight degree, these conditions will affect others in the immediate vicinity. They may experience feelings of depression, and the sensation of a cloudy atmosphere; but the thoughts are too unorganised to have a lasting effect, unless one is continually living with this species of thought emanation; it will not affect anybody seriously, EXCEPT the THINKER. He, or she, will at once show the work they have been unconsciously performing—bad digestion, sleepless nights, wrinkles, flabby cheeks, and the general inability to enjoy anything. These are the lasting results of such disturbance of the etheric substances.

We are all anxious to obtain success in life, and to help others; but the life success must be so perfectly blended with the spiritual success, that the two are one, else neither will be very lasting. I am aware that certain people may take exception to this statement, but it is my firm opinion that true life success embraces this dual aspect I have described.

The law of vibration is always travelling from a higher to a lower rate and back again; it follows a free-path motion, and returns upon its journey laden with the errand it set out to perform. If you will look at the first diagram of this lesson, you will see a perfect circle, which we will call the sphere of spirit. At the mark "A" in this circle we see pure spirit, and at "B" we will place matter. Thus "A," pure spirit, is a rate of vibration which is intense—

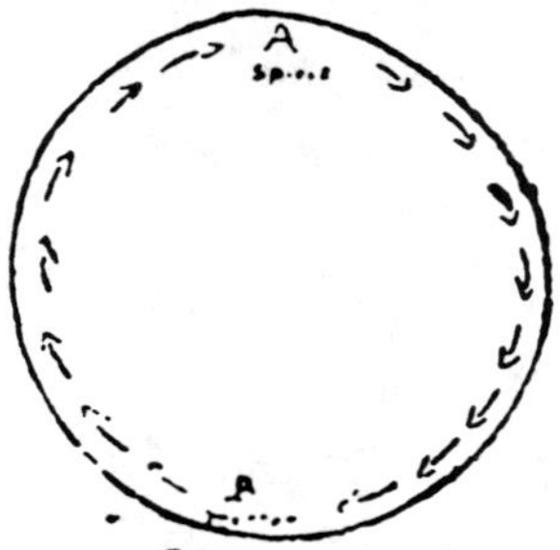

Fig I

(LESSON II.)

the swiftest possible. From this, spirit travels at a rate that grows slower and gradually slower, and, of course, more dense, until it arrives at the base "B," where it is practically at a standstill. This may be interpreted as the procession of spirit through the grosser shades of matter, until at "B" we find matter almost pure and simple; but from "B" back to "A" again this etheric flow grows swifter and swifter, until at "A" it again assumes its swiftest rate of speed, and, having shaken off the confining elements of matter, is again merged into pure spirit.

We can trace this as the process of life. All life is spirit, and this diagram represents the entire period from the first separation of the individual from spirit, on its journey through life to the time when, having passed through countless incarnations, it is ready to return whence it came. The reason for this journey is not apparent, it is simply the law of Nature.

Thus from "A" to "B" is the spiritual basis upon which we are all founded, and from which, by the slow processes of evolution, we attain the state of so much gross matter, the state in which quite nine-tenths of the population of the world are at present. Then, from here, man's higher sense begins to crave for a higher state of evolution, and at last realises that he has it in his power to obtain this when he pleases. "We live in that state of development our thoughts create for us." The higher our mental aspirations, the swifter and purer the rate of vibration we attain. If you live in the dirt you cannot expect to attract anything else; but if you are a child of sunshine, so will you be garbed in light, and draw to yourself all that is yours by right.

To retrace our steps a little, we will repeat that the brain centre is a medium, a machine for manifesting and creating thought, as a dynamo, only, of course, more powerful than any other known machine, and more perfect.

At the centre of the brain, energy is so intense that it almost appears to be still and calm, and from this still centre radiates outward thought, the quality and quantity of which depends upon the machine which generates the power. The generating process takes place through the all-compelling action of the WILL or OVER SOUL, that part of man which never dies. This action is helped, and often to a very great degree, by correct breathing, which has the most wonderful effect upon concentration of thought.

The following diagrams will illustrate very clearly how thought will proceed under given circumstances. Thought is dynamic, or, properly speaking, kinetic ; * but, of course, the words apply to the same thing. Under the compulsion of a strong and well-advanced WILL, or over soul, thought travels in a direct line towards that upon which it is concentrated. The more intense this form of concentration, the swifter and more direct the journey of that thought.

Fig. 2 shows the action of thought when directed upon some particular point. From "A" to "B" we get concentrated thought travelling from the brain

---

* "Producing motion. Force of any kind as a motive power and its action."

centre, " A," to the point it is intended to reach, " B." This may be defined as organised thought, a substance of which the vibrations are almost as subtile as the transmitting medium, etheric waves.

From " A " to " C," however, we obtain the action of thought as it is understood in every-day parlance,

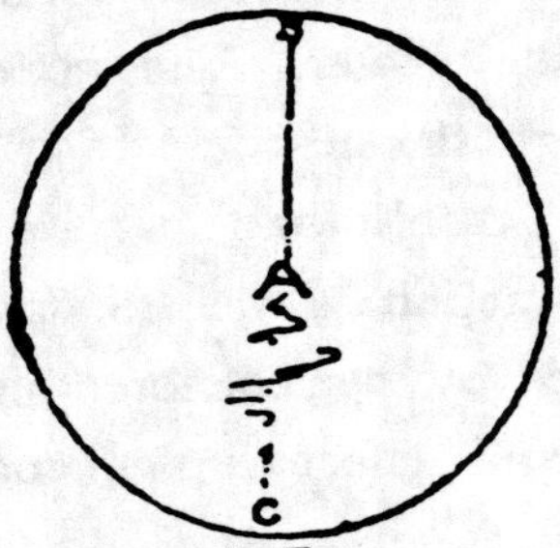

Fig. II

(LESSON II.)

the vacillating, uncertain thought of the unorganised mind which follows a zigzag course, varying in strength, and finally filtering away, without ever reaching its goal.

LESSON III

To resume the consideration of the various kinds of thought waves we will now consider Fig. III. (Lesson III.), which shows the action of the brain when generating another kind of mind wave, when the thought field, which closely resembles the magnetic field, as known to electricians, is composed of lines of force which are less concentrated because more scattered in area, since they radiate outwards to all points, still from the same calm centre.

But under the action of an organised mentality each line reaches the mark.

Thus from "A" to the outermost circle on every side, which in this case we will take to represent the known universe, or perhaps better still, as the world, the thought rays travel in even quality, and with direct force. When the student sits for general concentration, desiring, or expecting some good thing which mankind or nature as a whole (because of his relation to nature) can give him, but without specifying any individual, then his thought follows the direction of this figure, and his brain machine just *radiates* the thought as the sun radiates light.

It falls gently, and equally distributed upon all,

and almost insensibly, often by what may seem the queerest chances, those on whom it falls are drawn to that centre power, and the thinker, be it for business, or otherwise, realises that his concentration has borne fruit.

Figure IV. clearly indicates the nature of thought sent in the general direction, but consisting of

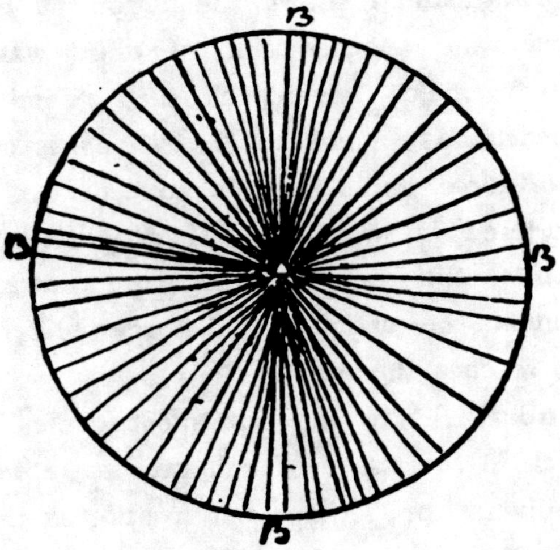

FIG. 3.

uneven and vacillating action, and will explain better than anything else why it is that some people have never achieved anything by the study of mental and spiritual science, or any other of the many methods of improving thought life.

They are not the masters of the laws governing mental action, nor do they clearly comprehend the kinetic nature of this curious and powerful substance, or the method of its propulsion through the ether.

The third law of motion is, "that action and reaction are equal in force, but opposite in direction."

Here we are considering the action of somebody endowed with energy by natural or mechanical means. As an example, if you take an india-rubber

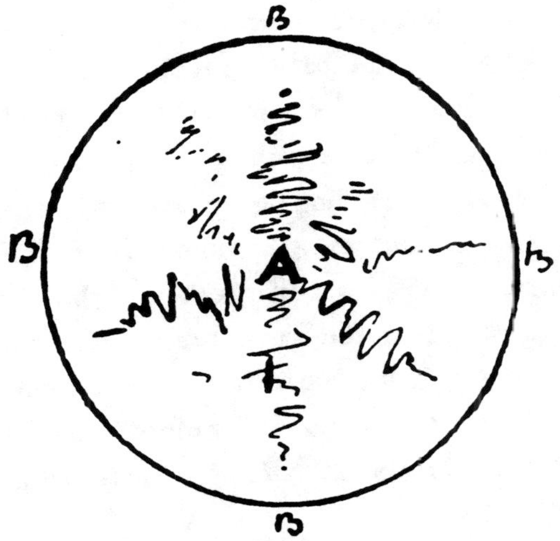

FIG. 4

ball and throw it against a wall, it will return to you with exactly the same force with which it struck the wall; and it's just exactly the same with any other body, or mass of atoms (for do not forget that everything from a stone to the human body is built up of atoms. In some things, such as the human body, gases, electricity, or water, the atoms are in continual motion; in others, such as rocks, certain chemicals. etc., they are in a state known as "inertia," that is to say, they are resting, waiting for some other substance to come along and wake them up, then, hey, presto! they are as full of life and energy as anything else. Often the chemical action of smoke and atmosphere will make large buildings, which are apparently dead, or inert, really a mass of movement, every tiny particle of stone vibrating), they come back to you with exactly the same force you send them, or with which nature sends them, as the case may be.

So that, say, the flinging of the ball against the wall is the action, and the force with which they meet creates the reaction, sending the ball back whence it came; at the same time if the ball strikes the wall so feebly that hardly any reaction is given, it will fall to the ground for want of momentum, or impetus *(the force with which a body is driven or impelled)*.

Thought rays (thought being a vibratory mass, as we have agreed) sent out through the ether with direct force, will return upon their centre (the brain) with equal force to that which sent them forth. So, according to this law, thought goes out, charged with its duty, and returns to the starting point having fulfilled its mission, if the thinker is organised. So that thought goes out to perform an errand, and will return to you laden with just what you sent it for, IF YOU ARE MASTER. *Thought is your* SERVANT, and if properly used will always bring you what you send it for.

In the realm of occultism the psychic forces which are used by man follow very much the same laws which govern the natural, or partly material world, but so far from realising this important fact man has sought for laws outside those he knows. It has been my experience that the occult is so simple it passes the comprehension of the man in the street, who looks for mystery where there really is none. Life in all its manifestations is simple, and is governed, as the ancients taught, by ONE life, ONE law, ONE word. It is the teachings which are complex, not the subject, and anything which can be done to simplify such teachings is most decidedly a step in the right direction.

There is the old, old motto, used by Freemasons and others of religious and mystic persuasions, *in hoc signo vinces* (by this sign thou shalt conquer), and man has speaking also of the esoteric societies and masonic brotherhood, taken this to mean the sign of the cross. Yet how can a cross help us to conquer? I will tell you what it really means, it is not the cross, but the CHRIST which will help us to conquer, and it is not even the Christ who is but a myth to many, it is the Christ within ourselves, and until we recognise this great power of good within us we shall never conquer. It has always seemed to me that the solidity of our bodies has been a drawback to the mental acceptance of the occult truths we are trying to make a part of our minds, and that the idea that we have so many stone of flesh and blood, bone and muscle to support, keeps us from the realisation of the mighty truth that we are all MIND and LOVE, so I am anxious for my pupils to get their minds clear of that and to believe and understand that they are as much spirit as anything else. The very materiality of the fleshly body is a hindrance to mental and psychical development, but I do not wish you to deny your body, it is there all right enough, and a very great necessity, too; I only want you to grasp the fact that by recognising the occult significance of "I AM LOVE," or "I AM POWER," you are admitting the fact that your entire body is *permeated throughout with the etheric waves which act as a medium for all things throughout the infinite.*

So that you ARE love and power, and being all love nothing can ever really harm you if you understand the law. Your body is an animated magnet, and the space it fills in the atmosphere is just a *great centre of attraction*. Say so half a hundred times a day, think of all it means to you, "I *am* FORCE, the LAW OF LIFE. The law is manifesting in my body and can be tapped for use whenever I wish to do so."

There is a great power in words, not that the words themselves are of any value, but they can and do convey suggestions, and when you concentrate upon certain words you set up the conditions those words convey to your brain machine. You say the word LOVE; it at once awakens a certain train of thought, and as you think you set in motion vibrations which, ever reaching outward, bring you into mental contact with the best the world has for you, the best part of the men and women with whom you come into business or social relations, the best of the mineral, animal, and vegetable kingdoms, and last, but not least, the best of the spiritual world and of YOURSELF. You MAKE yourself LOVE, and you are love; you simply radiate love as a stove or the sun radiates heat. So let that be your battle-cry; let it be your password to a better state, "I AM LOVE, LOVE FILLS MY ENTIRE BODY." Even if it brought you no material benefit (which it will do), the experiment is well worth trying for the simple pleasure of seeing how everybody you meet will unbend to your influence, and how much loved in return you will become. It will be simply your mental body responding to the suggestion carried by the word love, and from the mental to the physical body is but a gradation, and thus you manifest the meaning of this little word not only mentally, but physically.

I have shown how thought does and should travel, and why it is capable of performing its journey through the ether, but I only treated of this in a perfunctory manner, because I wanted to explain more fully in the lesson of thought fields, to which we are coming in our next lesson.

LESSON IV

THE arguments advanced in this lesson are worthy of particular attention, because, in the first place, they will help us to a clearer understanding of the occult power of thought when properly directed and *energised* by concentration, and also because it clearly demonstrates the affinity existing between esoteric and physical laws. Before treating of the effects of radiant energy and thought fields, it will be as well to understand, first, what radiant energy is, and second, what is a field?

To take the meaning of *energy* first, as distinguished from *motion;* energy is the term applied to any mass (or any *body*), which, when moving, strikes against another body and sets that also moving, and the power of the original body to move another is known as its *energy*, and measured according to the amount of movement it is able to impart.

Radiant energy is the term applied to any mass or body of matter possessing energy of a nature that can be imparted to the atmosphere, or the medium which surrounds it, and the speed with which this energy is transmitted depends entirely upon the ability of the medium to transmit energy, and not upon the *force* itself.

Thus the thought atoms are in perfect sympathy with the medium, ether, and as a consequence ether is an ideal transmitter for thought waves.

Remember that any substance or matter thus distributing radiant energy can set other masses of matter in motion, and this is an important part of our statement regarding the vibratory nature of thought. The ether transmits such wave motions in

FIG. 1.

straight lines and there is no limit to the distance they can travel, they can go on indefinitely; but the point I am leading up to is what is technically called the *field*, and the explanation thereof.

To return to my old method of illustration, I will ask you to look carefully at Fig. 1.

The centre "A" is the mass which we know possesses the power of distributing radiant energy. Now all the space outside that mass or body, to the extent within which it is capable of acting in this way upon other bodies, so as to bring them to a similar condition to its own, is what scientific men call *the field.* That is to say, the space surrounding and in front of the mass forms the field. So that "B" in the preceding diagram represents that *field;* and the *extent* of the field depends altogether upon the *force*, or energy, possessed by the mass. The more force it has the wider is the *field* through which its energy is distributed. Think how the great brains of the world make their influence felt. Or think again how the sun's energy pervades the vast space separating it from our planet.

Taking the magnet sun as the best possible illustration of an object akin to thought energy, it is known that a magnetic field cannot exist without an inducing magnet, or current of electricity. Every magnet has what are called its poles, the term applied to the two ends, and these poles are called respectively positive and negative. Magnetism as a study is probably unknown to many of my readers, and a few words of explanation may help the student. The common magnet or lode-stone is found in Magnesia, in Asia Minor, and in other parts of the world. It has the property of drawing, or attracting to itself pieces of steel and iron, and also of invariably pointing to the *north* and *south.*

Artificial magnets are made by rubbing a piece of steel on a lode-stone, when the iron will acquire the properties of the lode-stone. Dr. Gilbert, in 1600, found out that the attraction appeared to reside in a long-shaped magnet at two ends, and these two regions were called poles (Greek *polos*, from *pelo*, to move), so the magnetic pole is literally one of the points in a magnet, corresponding to the poles of the earth, the one pointing north and the other south; the poles are almost invariably at the ends. That portion of a magnet lying between the poles is less magnetic, and does not attract so strongly, and half way between the poles there is no attraction at all.

The first law of magnetism is that "like magnetic poles repel one another, and unlike magnetic poles attract one another." So that two north pointing poles will violently repel one another, but two poles, one north pointing, or positive, and the other south pointing, or negative, will attract one another.

The earth is itself a magnet with its north pointing and south pointing pole, and man is a magnet also; in fact all nature in its variety of forms and phases is composed of magnets, each atom and molecule having its positive and negative poles.

The human brain has also its positive and negative aspects, and its *poles* are situated respectively in the *cerebrum* and *cerebellum*, as the third diagram will show you (see Lesson I. for explanation of brain divisions). Figure 2 shows the ordinary magnetic lines radiating from an ordinary magnet, the space filled with the lines being the magnetic field.

Now coming to our immediate subject, *Thought*. You will readily understand how the THOUGHT FIELD can follow the same lines as the magnetic field. Here is the brain and the THOUGHT FIELD. Thus we get "A," the brain, "B," the thought lines the

FIG. 2.

thought field. As I explained before, there must be a body, or mass of matter to distribute radiant energy, and unless there is the body or *force* to create a field—magnetic, electric, chemical, mechanical or *thought*, which you please—there can be no field.

In the *thought field* the BRAIN is the mass of matter, the force which radiates energy and creates a "*field;*" in the feeble, unorganised brain this field is weak, and affects only a limited area. But the greater the personal magnetism, the more powerful and organised the brain, the greater the extent of its radiation, the wider its field, the more lasting its effects. And the generation of ***thought force***, or mind, which I described in my last lessons, makes the advent of some great man or woman. Great, according to the sphere of their labour and their ruling talent.

Thus, roughly, we have Christ, Buddha, Nero,

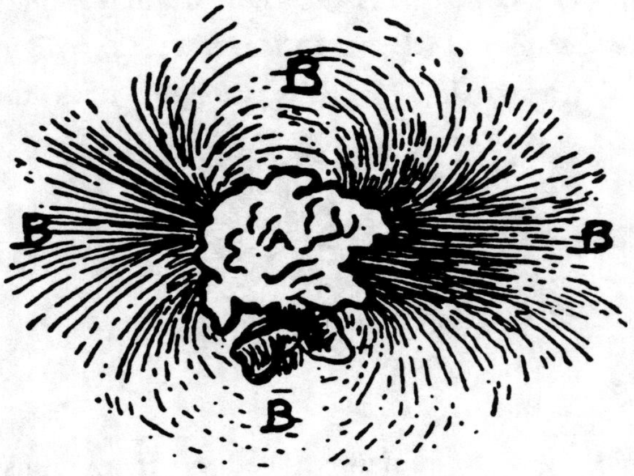

FIG. 3.

Shakespeare, Boadicea, just a few names, with different qualities, yet all with sufficient ***force*** to have created energy enough to last through the ages!

all were leaders.
had a definite vision,
and this energised themselves
to energise others

When two brains are working together for the purposes of telepathy, or healing, one must be positive, the other negative, and they create what is called ***attraction***, for by means of the sympathy between them they set up a stress (pressure) in the ether, and the thought fields act in such a way that they are pushed together (by this I mean the thought lines, not the brains), and commingle and blend under the conditions described above. They exchange, or transfer their energy, the transfer always taking place from the one possessing the higher rate to the one possessing the lower. Thus one person

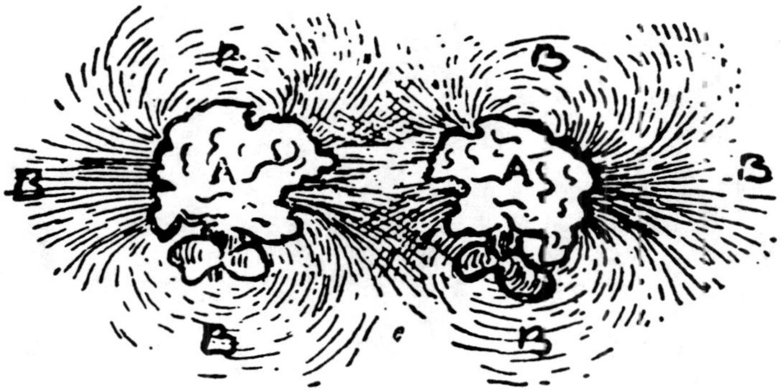

FIG. 4.

acts as a transmitter, and the other as a receiver. The one is *negative*, and the other *positive*, otherwise they would *repel* instead of *attract*, since "like magnetic poles repel one another, and unlike magnetic poles attract." That is to say, two positive poles would repel each other, but a positive pole and a negative pole would attract each other. So like minds repel each other, and unlike minds attract, or

This is why you get on so well - you are on the 'same wavelength' as people you are friendly with.

perhaps it would be better to say that the strong mind attracts the weak, and *vice versâ*.

Illustration 4 shows how each brain acts upon the thought field of the other, and it should be remembered this action applies more particularly to the various processes of mental healing, success vibration, etc., etc.

LESSON V

WE must not forget that the attributes of the mass are possessed by the atom (that is to say, each atom contains in itself everything to be found in the mass), and that every atom of brain matter or of thought is acting upon each neighbouring atom in the same way that one brain will act upon another, and that this is going on indefinitely, so that every object throughout the cosmos is continually affecting the space surrounding it in various ways, its temperature (thought HAS a temperature, and to the sensitive this becomes at once apparent, whether hot, cold or normal, and it is my opinion that a machine will soon be made showing the thought temperatures of people), and its effects upon the surrounding space, with its magnetic or electric qualities, and in the case of thought with its spiritual, material, good and mistaken qualities.

It is because of the vastness of thought and its possibilities that the study of its laws is so interesting and so very complex. When a man makes a movement of his body, he at once alters the position of the ether, and sets up a stress or pressure; but when he thinks, he sets up a much more powerful stress;

and when we consider the thinking which characterises some minds, we can at once understand why they are like a rudderless boat in a stormy sea; they seem to be setting up all sorts of cross currents around them, and the result is a life of misery. When the organised thinker exercises mental power, he sets up an even stress, and, to use a simile, the wind only blows one way, and so this man is not literally devoured by his own conflicts. I do not think that any man would willingly attempt to make his life hell, when he can make it heaven to a very great extent. To show how deeply we are affected by the thoughts of others, consider a clever actress; she can play upon the feelings of her audience, move them to tears, horror, or laughter, just as she pleases, yet her mental state is only simulated; but for the time the greater number of that audience are really CONCENTRATING on the woman before them, and so are swayed by the emotions she depicts.

So I get my pupils to concentrate on what they love to begin with. That is why, as a general rule, people who take up the new thought can rout poverty quicker than any evil of the body. They are fairly used to sickness, etc., but they can never feel satisfied with the continual grind of poverty.

If you emit love, you will shake off that demon

hate; if you think only of success you will gain it; BUT if you give your heart to these things only you will succeed for a *time* only. Bear in mind that the voice of the Spirit must be obeyed also, and that before you can achieve earthly happiness you must be equally advanced in both spiritual and material things.

Man is mechanical, and his development to a certain plane is also mechanical, but after that the *mind man* holds full sway, and we can become just what our minds conceive, ordered only by such laws of nature as are part of our being, and intended for our general unfoldment. It is true, as mental science claims, that we can overcome evil and substitute good, but we can never be quite free from nature's laws, and the very mistakes we make are prime factors in our mental development.

In the previous lessons we have been chiefly concerned with the projection of thought in a concentrated form, and passing on to the consideration of personal and curative magnetism, we will investigate the methods of concentrating our forces within.

That is to say, instead of projecting our thought outward to either convey a message, bring back an answer, or to attract certain affinities we desire from out the infinite, we are now thinking of turning our thought forces inwards, and must contrive to do so in such a manner that no outward radiation takes place whatever.

I am assuming the student to be aware that all force comes from within, and that all spirit is also within; that is to say, there is no need to "prospect" outside the self. Within your own physical body are contained all your psychic forces, and also your *spiritual body*, whilst locked up in the memory of the past are all the teachings of spirit, all knowledge of life and so-called death, of love, of truth, of power, all that has ever been—you know it all; you have but to unlock the memory of past births and you will speedily find that before you is a store of knowledge such as you never imagined possible before.

To a certain extent we are ordered by destiny, yet so far as the general events of each incarnation are concerned we are alone responsible for them. Each man and woman is a power in themselves, possessing all the potentiality of divinity. They need not seek for light from without; they have it all within themselves.

This is the most difficult lesson the student has to learn; it is curious that he may read it in hundreds of books, be told it by as many teachers, but until he has arrived at a certain stage of development he cannot realise the fact for what it is worth.

This method of inward concentration is the most precious of all and the most important. The processes I have indicated in previous lessons appertain more to the acquirement of material things than spiritual, but this method applies more nearly to the realm of spirit.

I do not wish to be misunderstood. All thought, as all progress, comes from within, but under certain circumstances you project that thought, and under certain other circumstances it is turned inward, so that all the light of your reason is concentrated upon your soul.

When we project our thoughts we send them outside ourselves, maybe to travel on some mission, or to heal the sick, to carry a message to a friend, or any other material object, good in itself, but not always of the highest spiritual benefit—to the thinker. If you will look at illustration 1 (Lesson V.) you will see the method involved. The outermost circle may be regarded as the limit of the brain; of course, meaning the machine, not the force generated.

This circle I have marked "B." "A" is the physical heart, the altar of the etheric centres of the body (according to the Rosicrucian teachings). Now the rays of thought, instead of being projected outwards, are turned directly inwards to the heart, and these rays, or vibrations, follow the direction of

"B" to "A," instead of from "A" to "B." So that, like a dark lantern, there is nothing to be seen from outside, all the light is concentrated within.

As in the ordinary form of concentration, do not try too much at first. This is even more trying than the other, because, unless a very ardent student of the occult, it is less interesting. At the same time, where true progress is desired it is absolutely necessary.

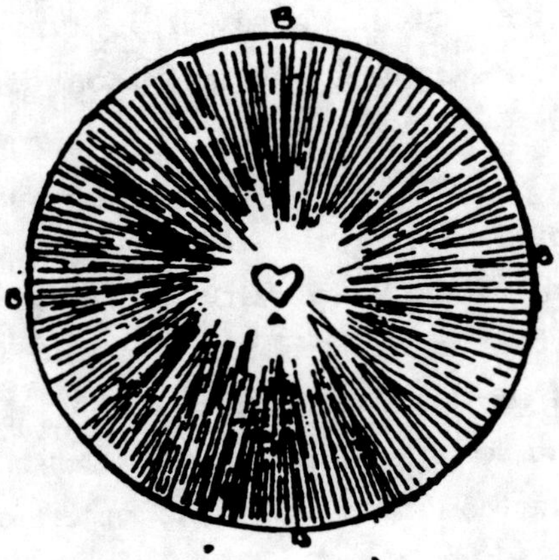

Fig I ([illegible])

As long as we learn from books and from lessons we are but novitiates, and the knowledge we obtain is second hand at best, but once we have really learnt how to concentrate we no longer remain in the outer temple, we are no longer dependent upon others, we *know for ourselves*. Study the foregoing diagram well; then, having got the idea firmly in your mind, sit down quietly and turn your thoughts inwards as I have described.

I find that pupils are more likely to achieve results if they use some word or words in their concentration, and suggest the following:

Breathe deeply, but perfectly evenly and without effort; do not attempt to count the breathing, nor to hold it any length of time; let the whole process be quite natural and not forced. Deep breathing, that is to say from the abdomen, or rather from behind it, from the solar plexus, has a most curious and direct effect upon all efforts in the way of concentration, clairvoyance and kindred powers of spirit.

As you breath in, think; ***think***, with every particle of your brain, "*Love.*" Consider, as you say it, all that is bound up in the word, how it relates you to spirit. "I have always been love; I am love divine, and I intend to manifest my divinity in this body." Dwell upon this as you take your inhalation, and as you slowly and evenly exhale.

Keep on repeating this for from five to ten minutes. "Love," or "Wisdom," "Life," "Divinity," but you must think it up with all your mind and continue to do so until you have taken it in in its entirety. You must soak it in, and when you have got it, keep fast hold, and do not ever relinquish.

When you think these words you are gradually moulding yourselves into these conditions. Perhaps the best word of all is "Power"; it means so much, but you must clearly realise *what* you do mean, and you must not take up any side issues, nor let your thoughts wander from the inward focus I have described. That is why I gave the other forms of concentration first, because they are easier to master, and prepare the student for the heavier task now under discussion. Remember that your thought can mould your body, and that as you think so you will become, so that when you stop for ten minutes or longer in the contemplation of your prospective power, wisdom and love, you are actually growing into these things, and as long as you think them intelligently you are bound to become them.

Now when you have accomplished this matter, try a little farther; but although you take all the lessons at once, you cannot do both these exercises at once, and you simply must take one step at a time.

Sit as before, breathe evenly; now ask a question, make your mind blank, and listen for the answer. You will get a clear message in perhaps a month or two. Do not be impatient, you cannot hurry this thing; just listen as if you were waiting for a human voice to speak to you. Listen intently, and at last you will get an answer, either directly or as an impression.

It is very difficult for some people to make the brain a blank, and it is not at all easy to teach the process. I think, however, that the best way is to take it by degrees. Try to kill all thought for a minute at a time, gradually increasing the time, from day to day. In this way you obtain perfect control of your brain machine. You can eliminate thought altogether or think on any chosen subject at will, and you must not despair if you do not gain immediate results. You cannot possibly learn in a second, it takes time, and the longer you take to acquire your knowledge the more thorough it will be, and the results more lasting.

LESSON VI

THERE are two distinct aims in the attainment of the power of concentration. First, to mould the consciousness into a new and better state; second, to attain the highest possible knowledge of things spiritual.

Remember that habit is what you desire to cultivate, so that you are able to form your body anew, and to repeat the process almost involuntarily is the chief necessity for continual and regular concentration, for the more concentrated and single your mind becomes on any particular point, the more it tends to permanency, and in the same way, if you are irregular, you tend to suppress the thought power you ought to manifest.

The cellular brain tissues are greatly changed by this process of correct thinking, and may be actually increased, whilst those which have been constructed by wrong thinking are caused to waste away. Every effort at right thought, or concentration, brings into play a new set of atoms which tend to build up the new tissues, and at the same time devour and destroy the old.

There is absolutely nothing in all the world so

plastic as the brain of man. It can be moulded by the will or over soul of the owner or of someone who may have influence over him, and in this way a teacher, by applying the right impulse, may bring the pupil to a higher state of mind, and help him in the process of rebuilding his physical and mental system.

When a man arrives at a state when he realises how much his over soul can do for him, he does not need a teacher to help in the moulding process, but when, as very frequently happens, the spirit awakens in a man whose over soul is still more or less dormant, then is the guidance of a teacher more or less of a necessity.

Often the searcher after truth doubts his own power and divinity, and so long as he doubts he will obtain little benefit from the occult. It is the poor opinion of his own powers which keeps man in the background, and also that he forgets that every moment of his life he is fashioning the future, that is to say, that all his thoughts to-day may take material form to-morrow, or the day after, so that each time he fails to concentrate with earnest purpose, each time he omits the daily exercise, he is postponing his future happiness.

The action of breathing deeply, which I have recommended, has the effect of quickening the circulation of the blood, and in some way acts upon the brain tissue, making sight, in the spiritual sense, hearing, and sense all more acute; and when you think some strong and positive thought as you breathe, it has the effect of sending this message to every part of the body, right along the nerves, arteries and blood vessels, until the whole body has taken up the chorus and is full of the power of your thought. Here again the value of concentration comes in; a decided message sent along your physical telegraph wires reaches the point at once and makes a firm and decided record, whilst a weak thought has no such effect. So that if you seek to overcome some bodily ill, get a clear grasp of the part that needs renovation, and then turn all your thought force inwards and send a strong message to that part.

"I am strong, I am well, I am divine. All is life, and in my thought and mind dwells infinite life. I am making my future all along the line, and that future shall be perfection. I am invincible, nothing can harm me, and it is my intention to manifest my power right now in my body."

Do not say these words like a parrot; think of all they mean, think of all they put behind you, and of all they open up before you. You are making your future now, *Now*, and when you sit in concentration you are weaving your own fate—good, bad or indifferent.

Having learnt how to concentrate for a few minutes at a time, first on things mundane, then on the more difficult phases of spirit, make a habit of devoting a short time daily to the contemplation of your future prospects. When you begin to know the peace and calm which falls upon you after sitting in this concentration, you will begin to value it accordingly; at first it soon wears off, but as your mind becomes more and more organised so will the results last longer, and the time will come when you can take this infinite peace with you wherever you go, take it with you and bestow it upon others.

In the natural course of events all the thought force which I am asking you to conserve is wasted, and so you achieve little success in either business or any other matter.

When you desire business success you must concentrate all your thought force upon the matter that must succeed, and you must then name it aloud; in your thought see it a success, and then expect that success to manifest.

Now having done that, begin to weave your thought into powerful currents. See these currents travelling to the object and surrounding it on every side, until it is bathed in powerful currents of thought force.

which are more powerful and can travel faster than a flash of lightning, and are more deadly in execution than a strong electric battery; these in their turn act as magnets and attract all the good forces in other people who are brought into contact with the matter in hand, and they in their turn do all they can to foster its success. You may ask how to weave the thought current I have spoken of.

I strongly advise the use of the imagination to aid in this. The first ingredient is the power to concentrate; the second is to see in your imagination

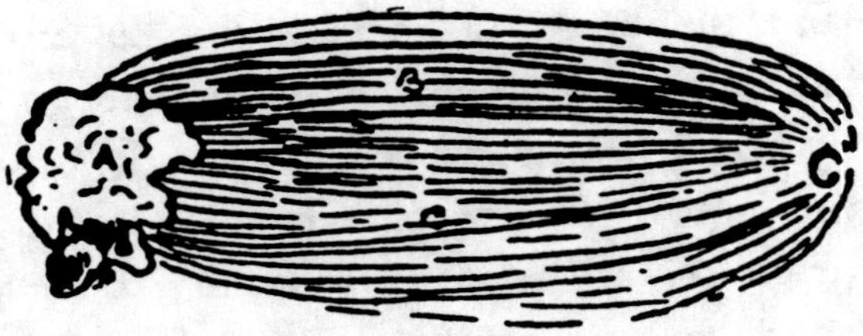

your mind machine producing and generating a very fine and subtle fluid, full of this marvellous power; then, of course, you project it as directed in the first lesson, and let it follow the course given in the above diagram. "A" is the brain, "B" is the thought force which travels on its journey through the ether, "C" is the object you desire to enfold with this mighty current of living mind stuff.

Perform this exercise two or three times a day, and you will never fail, that is to say, as soon as you have got your brain into a sufficiently organised condition to carry out your orders. This ought to be the case in about two or three months, if you follow these lessons implicitly. You see, it is not a case of miracles, but simply a system of organised education, and the results are as sure as the Tower of London.

Always regard thought as a substance. You can conceive very easily of the effect a flash of lightning would have if it played around any given object for a time, or better still, you well know the effect a current of magnetism has upon a bar of iron, and as I have told you again and again, your thought is more powerful than any of these things, and when you play it in the right condition around any given object, then you produce the same results; for as the flow of magnetism produces what is known as induction *(that is to say, the transference of a magnetic or electric state from an electrified body to a non-electrified body, by proximity without contact)*, so your thought force inducts its etheric substance into whatever you choose to play it upon.

The analogies between the science of electricity, and, indeed, the whole realm of physics and the noumenal world of thought and spirit are curious, and the more one investigates the more certain it appears that the same laws govern both.

LESSON VII

THESE papers would not be perfect without some reference to the method of concentration used by the Indian adepts, who acquire the habit ONLY BY DEVOTING A LIFETIME TO THE STUDY. We in the West have not the time for this, nor do I think we shall benefit very much by the various methods of "killing thought" advocated by those who wish merely to make the mind blank to receive inspirational communications from what is the "unknown," but I know that we can make our mind blank without any particular effort if we will not attempt to do too much at first; and we must also remember that strong healthy bodies are necessities for those who would take up the concentrating methods with any zest, for when we hold our mind to any given subject for any length of time, the grosser atoms of thought which have travelled to the spot or object concentrated upon, sink down, back to the original starting place—in fact they filter away, and their place is taken by finer particles, causing a great mental strain upon the thinker, and unless there is strong health to back up the nervous strain, madness, or brain fever would be the result, but as long as the health is all right concentration will benefit, and not harm the student. Grow to the practice gradually, and you will gain all you need, and find all efforts crowned with success.

It is not at all a bad plan to use a glass bowl of water when concentrating. Fix the desire in mind, and try to see the words spell out in the bowl; this method helps to fix the attention, and if a bowl of water is not handy, try a pencil and a piece of paper; the idea is simply to convey the message to the brain, through the retina of the eye, for this holds the image as does the sensitive plate used by the photographer.

Sit when most convenient—it is almost impossible to have any fixed time. In any course of lessons written for general use it is almost impossible to give just the information needed by each individual, and if my pupils will explain their personal difficulties they will help me and themselves, for I will gladly write a full reply to all their requirements upon receipt of 2s. 6d. to cover time and stationery.

The following brief rules may be remembered:—

If you want money, see it coming to you; let your concentration be general; have faith; expect what you want to come to you.

If you have ill health, do not think of the particular disease which may trouble you, but concentrate all your attention upon the acquirement of perfect health; do not let any other idea come into your mind for the time being; say, "*I AM WELL, PERFECT HEALTH IS MINE, pure vital blood flows through my veins; I am a perfect manifestation of the All Good, and in every part of my body there is nothing but life and love.*" I have found this statement to bring relief even in the most obstinate cases, and it seldom fails. Talk nothing but health, sleep, dream, and EAT it, and you will very soon manifest it, for if people talked health half as assiduously as they discuss their pet ailments, the doctors would have to find a new profession!

Do you think that because you have not immediate health that you are making a false statement; you are, by your mental attitude, preparing the "TO-MORROW," and so the statement is true, for if you say "I will be well," instead of "I am well," you are postponing the harvest of your thought.

If your trouble should be some great sorrow let your statement run thus:—"*I AM LOVE, LOVE FILLS MY BODY, AND I AM FULL OF THE GLORIOUS AND JOYOUS RADIANCE ONLY LOVE CAN EMIT. ALL IS GOOD, AND I AM HAPPY.*" Do not say this once but dozens of times, and allow the statement to sink in until you become the image of your ideal.

In time you will become as radiant as the love you profess, and when this takes place you will find the world all right without any further effort on your part.

Now I intend passing on to the subject of "Personal Magnetism," and the question naturally arises:—

What *is* Personal Magnetism?

Followed by the equally pertinent demand—What are its *uses?*

Personal Magnetism is really many things. First it is organised *will power;* secondly it is *health;* thirdly it is the ability to amalgamate the will power and health, and aided by the desire to "*obtain*" certain objects, to so *project* the subtile and highly potent magnetic force thus generated in the body, as to attract people and circumstances—it means that every man and woman can become a natural magnet, if they will persevere in their efforts to develop this force.

As for its uses, they are many.

This magnetic force is powerful to heal the sick, the greatest use to which, in my opinion, it can be put.

It enables the man or woman who possesses it to *attract* or *repel* at will, or to draw to themselves SUCCESS, MONEY, FAME, POWER, HAPPINESS *(if they use it wisely)!*

Animal magnetism, then, is a very subtile substance filling the entire universe.

It is more subtile than *ether*, just as ether is more subtile than air, and air than water.

As the vibrations of the ether permit light to travel, and the vibrations of the air sound, so the vibrations of the animal magnetism permit and cause other phenomena.

This vibratory substance is sometimes called "*od*" or "*odylic force*," but I prefer the term animal or personal magnetism, because it is so much simpler and easier to understand, whether it is to be used as a healing agent or for any other purpose.

Every magnet has a ***positive*** and ***negative*** pole (the poles are situated at the two ends of an elongated magnet). These terms are generally accepted to mean—"*Positive*"—MORE, STRONGER, "*Negative*"—LESS, or WEAKER. The first law of Magnetism is that like Magnetic poles repel one another, and unlike Magnetic poles attract.

So the ***positive*** attracts the ***negative***, the ***negative*** the ***positive***, the ***strong*** the ***weak***.

In man, the Magnet, the two poles are represented by his body and mind, we are taught by Helen Wilmans.

The BODY is the ***negative pole***, MIND or THOUGHT POWER the ***positive***. The ***positive mind***, the ***mind*** *which has been made familiar with its own unlimited power*, can *attract to itself, by an ordinary reasoning process Animal Magnetism*, and *increase and store this force for every-day use, and generate it according to necessity.*

It is intimately associated with your *will power*, your *brain*, your *thought*, but for the cultivation you must follow the exercises given in a later lesson, and you will attain *real life*, will *throw off your years, off your cares*, and gain such *health and success* as you desire—and *more!*

The recognition of a Universal Intelligence is essential.

I want you to become strong Individually, to rest upon the knowledge of your own power; but do not forget this same power is but the reflected glory of the *one Light*, the centre of all things.

It is the custom of many teachers of Metaphysics to assert that a personal God is impossible, that God is an essence, and does not possess a personality.

With this teaching many pupils are repelled who would otherwise be attracted to the Higher Thought.

Science must always *advance*, and when I undertake the task of assimilating the metaphysical Deity with the Theological Deity, I am going one step forward.

Briefly the idea is this:—

It has been astronomically ascertained that the milky way is a gigantic belt of suns and worlds (of which our own Solar System is a very second rate affair, so far as size is concerned) which is continually revolving around, and is ordered by some unseen centre of Gravity, upon which the whole depends. This, I am firmly convinced is "*God*"—the Father, *a God* of *unlimited power*.

From this glorious Being radiates a powerful, subtile essence, which reaches throughout the unlimited realms of space — and the name of this emanation is both *Life* and *Love*.

Wherever there is substance or life, which it for ever creates—*there* is set up a *Holy Shrine*, and the place assigned to that shrine in man, is, by Rosicrucians, assumed to be the *physical HEART*, which is the centre of the physical body, as the Father is the centre of ALL.

Within the valves of the human heart this *Holy radiance settles and finds a home*, as a sunbeam might settle upon a flower, and from *thence*, at *the dictation of man's conscious will* and *thought*, this *Divine light can again radiate in infinite love*, *drawing to the man all he needs of health*, *or wealth*, *or happiness*. For in this way he becomes one with the Father, an intimate and dearly beloved Friend.

This definition may also be applied to the *brain*, if the student prefers that to the *physical heart*.

Now FAITH in your power to achieve success in the use of personal Magnetism is a very large factor towards that success.

The man who has confidence in his ability, when wishing to transmit Magnetism, is going a very long way towards swift results; but the man who *doubts his ability to exert this force simply wastes it.*

A state frequently seen in the idealistic mind is that of the dreamer who can formulate but never execute, simply because of either intense waste of Magnetic power, or because of prostration of the entire nervous system.

A strong will must be normal, having complete control over every mental and bodily function, and to this end these lessons are intended.

I am teaching you to assert your SELF to be an Individual Entity, instead of a knock-kneed invertebrate, bolstered up at every turn by all sorts of unhealthy, weakening devices. The Magnetic WILL can only be cultivated by constant practice, when instead of being the plaything of Fate or Circumstance, you become the wire-puller, and order your own Circumstance.

LESSON VIII

PERSONAL magnetism, then, means *power*, and the ability to exert that power over people, and even to a certain extent over circumstances, because the people we influence and come in contact with go a long way towards CREATING circumstances.

The man or woman best able to exert this power belongs to what is known as the VITAL temperament.

This, when analysed, resolves itself simply into the temperament of perfect health and vitality; although it is very usual to make this temperament a matter of colouring (red, or auburn haired people, in fact), I don't find it pans out this way at all, in fact, ANY colouring may be vital, provided the person has the energy and perseverance to cultivate the vital principles; and it's purely humbug to put any hard and fast rule to this matter at all.

The one thing that *is* certain, however, is that all *want* to cultivate that temperament who are desirous of obtaining POWER, TRUE LIFE and SUCCESS. Vital means LIFE or relating to life, and the vital temperament is used to describe those people who are in a state of PERFECT MENTAL AND PHYSICAL BALANCE.

They enjoy perfect bodily and mental health, and the one is ***not*** developed at the expense of the other

They have clear, fresh skins, bright eyes, firm flesh, spirits buoyant, and the power of attracting other people very great. These, in a word, are the people who possess the greatest store of NATURAL ***animal magnetism.***

But the great point is that one and all can take on this characteristic, and so increase their stock of magnetic and electric particles that they BECOME VITAL!

The vital temperament radiates magnetism.

The invisible currents pass off in every direction from every part of the body, and so great is the force of this subtle power, that although ***invisible to the naked eye the camera can reveal it;*** and the HUMAN BODY and HUMAN MIND at once feel the impression, bodily ***as a thrill,*** or ***sensation of warmth,*** mentally as an ***invigorating shock*** from an electric battery, or as an overpowering desire to "***go out and do something***"!

Such a temperament has the ability to influence every person (and animal) who comes in contact with him, but has a GREATER POWER THAN THIS.

He can influence those with whom he does not come into actual contact until they are drawn to him, in answer to his thought.

This man radiates his magnetic power in the spirit of UNIVERSAL LOVE. He recognises the spirit, or the love principle in everyone, shedding his power from the store-house I have described in Lesson VII. upon mankind as a whole.

The powerful magnetic rays issuing from his person draw to him, from out of the immense mass of humanity, all that can be useful to him.

He sees *within* himself the Love Spirit; he mentally sees this spirit radiating outward from his body an essence of immense force, which finds a resting place within those hearts, or upon those minds which he so lovingly recognises.

REMEMBER that the man or woman who misuses this power will surely find it turned back upon themselves to their undoing.

WHEN YOU ATTRACT PEOPLE it is because you supply something they need, something they lack; your powerful magnetism fills an empty space. This is the secret which makes one public speaker a huge success, and another a downright failure.

The one man has a great store of personal magnetism. He holds his audience enthralled, they listen to every word and are carried along by the mighty wave of his immense strength and MAGNETIC FORCE.

The other man has none. His words fall flat, his

hearers remain unmoved. Yet he may be a man of polish, of education, of rank, with the easy speech born of cultured ancestors; and the first man might be poor, uncultured, and of the people. But the first man knows his subject, believes in his power to attract, and by sheer will power carries his point.

IN BUSINESS MATTERS the same rule applies: the man of force, possessing this wonderful power of attraction, carries all before him. He is the man who can convince the unwilling (and be it said, unorganised) customer against his will. He is the man who can draw to himself success and DOLLARS in equal proportion, and can climb to the topmost rung of the ladder.

In the acquirement of this life, force applies to every grade of society and to BOTH SEXES.

The next point for consideration is how to generate the force.

To recognise your central spirit light is hardly enough; you must fan the flame, and generate fresh power, *concerning the forces you already possess.* Brain and nerve power are the secret forces. The brain is to be strengthened and developed and so are the nerves.

SELF-CONTROL is the first factor to be observed. You, sir, who cannot keep your hands still; you, madam, who are for ever patting your back hair, or pulling at your dress, or twisting your watch chain. You who start at every sound, who fidget and fume and worry over trifles, who are nervous and irritable, giving way to passion, and being but the plaything of circumstance, to you, I say, learn to control *self*, for all these mannerisms are resulting in a continuous and serious leakage of magnetism, which if used aright would enable you to COMMAND SUCCESS.

The "magnetic" people are fair with blue eyes, and pale or delicate skins. They are fidgety, nervous, often hysterical, and suffer as a rule from too great brain activity. Their mind is never at rest, they are continually worrying over trifles, and are of a cold, and often selfish temperament.

By control you can overcome these leakages, and by overcoming, stop them. So, by nerve and brain development—recognising the brain *always as the nerve centre, in connection with the ganglionic centres, at the base of the brain*—you can control the leakage and waste of magnetism, and so become magnetic.

The so called "electric" temperament, belonging to people who are generally dark in appearance, with sallow, or pale skins, having mental powers which are often sluggish, and a tendency to suffer from liver, laziness and similar complaints, requires plain, non-heating diet, very little meat—vegetarians are the healthiest; I never touch meat—regular hours, and last, but *not* least, in addition to the exercises given in a later lesson, regular mental exercise; they need arousing, and their brain needs stimulation. They need nourishing, heat-producing foods (not necessarily meat), and they also require a time when they can be *passive*, forcing themselves to either *less* brain activity, or else to concentrate on one subject only.

These two types can, however, by following the rules I shall give in subsequent lessons, become *vital* and live as they please, master of their conditions, instead of the conditions being master over them.

The object of the descriptions of the various temperaments is intended to help the student in his knowledge of life and people, and to be used practically in the development of power.

The successful man or woman is *master*, but cannot be master unless he or she has learned how to be *all things to all men.*

When you have developed your personal magnetism you also develop your power of selection to an enormous extent, and you realise at a glance which battery to use for those you come into contact with, in business or society.

Personal magnetism, once the power has been

developed, resolves itself into sympathy, the act of supplying to others elements they lack.

This you cannot supply voluntarily unless you are in a position to order and command your own forces.

Any man who has complete control over his entire physical and mental organism can hold the world enthralled in time as he enlarges his sphere of action. To the electric person you must supply electricity, stimulate their brains, probe them with questions to make them think, and they will be glad to always do your commands, because you have shown them a new side to their nature.

The magnetic people like to be soothed; some of them, too, do not care for things easily obtained; these people you must *repel*, show them the independent side of your nature, let them believe you would rather not have any dealings with them; only give in with decided reluctance.

The more you draw back, the more eager they become. Others again need persuasion—help. By mental suggestion you can make up their minds for them.

The mental rules are always as follows; dilute them, please, with three parts common sense, to one part rule or maxim. The physical rules will follow later.

You are conscious of your own strong magnetic power, and you are aware that you radiate this power, or substance, as the sun radiates light.

You have come into business intending to obtain success only, and you hold no doubt in your mind but that the other man will deal just exactly as you desire him to deal.

When dealing with people in business or society, hold your mind firmly to the power you possess, look them squarely in the face, and command them, mentally, to fulfil your desires. Think, "I am a man of organised power; I desire to carry such and such a plan into execution. Your brain is negative to mine, and I demand that you shall do so and so. I am master; I will have what I want."

You can supply this same magnetic order when writing a letter. Hold the letter in your hand, or to your forehead, and *will* that it shall come to such and such an issue.

Your magnetic battery exists within your own body; at the command of your *will* you can radiate and generate this force.

Will power is vital thought, or mind.

Magnetism, therefore, becomes a centre of communication between gross spirit or matter, and refined, or etherealised spirit or matter. Spirit is the eternal, active life principle, manifesting in all matter, as well as through the various *spheres of spirit*.

The force which moves the world, magnetism, may be represented in your mind in one word, *suggestion*, or the command of will power, ending in either the spoken word or *concentrated thought*, is the weapon you must use through life, and that as your power so you can act by suggestion upon one man, or one thousand men.

LESSON IX

In the *physical* exercises I give in these lessons it is as well to remember that very little good will result unless *proper breathing exercises* are indulged in, as well as the physical. Muscles alone are *not* the first consideration, and muscle does not really tend to promote personal magnetism. In moderation they are beautiful, but when overdone they transform the most perfectly formed man into a grotesque "something," that ought to be planed down with a carpenter's plane to reduce it to its proper proportions. Let the muscles be lithe and supple, like steel and whipcord; let the *lungs* be perfectly developed, so that they can create healthy blood, which is vitality, and let both be equally blended.

Dumb-bell exercises with *heavy* bells certainly tend to create muscle; but it is heavy, lumbering, useless, except for brute strength, so that the heaviest dumb-bells a man should use are 3 lb. bells, and a woman 1 lb.

Before commencing any exercises of a muscular nature, first learn how to control the breath. *Very* deep breathing is injurious, but most people exercise the lungs so slightly that they become atrophied—

waste away for want of use, because they are never properly filled or emptied!

Attitude is the first step of importance. You can't breathe if you round your shoulders and let your chin sink forward on your chest. Stand erect, waist in (in front, please, I must be polite, I suppose; but when I say *waist* I mean abdomen), shoulders squared and held back, chest well out, head thrown back, chin in. Now, with your mouth closed, draw a slow, deep breath (*not too deep at first, for by violent breathing the lungs only become tender and bruised*), hold it for a second, then as slowly exhale, or breathe out through the nostrils.

There are three methods of breathing: from the abdomen, or solar plexus, from the rib and from the upper chest. Begin right down in the abdomen—but gently, please—and draw the breath in through the nostrils so that the abdomen (don't forget the abdomen is not the stomach, the two are quite distinct; the stomach is the bag or receptacle for one's food; the abdomen, the thick fleshy wall which covers the intestines) is drawn in. In this way you force the intestines into action, awaken the solar plexus, and then slowly fill the lungs with fresh air, which in turn generates fresh blood, and fills every fibre and tissue of the body with new life—and ANIMAL MAGNETISM. This process done to excess will tire you, so be gentle at first, especially if you are one of those poor unfortunate wretches whose sole idea of breathing—if they ever think of it at all—is a little, quick, panting action which never fills the lungs once—nor empties them—and accounts *so* fully for pale cheeks, lifeless eyes, flabby flesh, and narrow pigeon breasts.

Proper action, proper breathing, perfect development, control of *will* power, and the acquirement by these means of perfect health and animal magnetism, are within the reach of *all.*

It may be urged that all people who possess this subtle power of magnetism, have *not* got perfect health.

Agreed, but they *have* perfect *will* control, and as a rule are absolute masters of some one or more accomplishment; and their magnetism is very apt to evaporate apart from the said accomplishment. Just *think* how few popular authors, painters or musicians are interesting, or even attractive, apart from their works.

No, *you simply must have* HEALTH, *an organised body as well as an organised* MIND, *if you are to fulfil* MY *ideal of personal magnetism.*

Given that, you may be as ugly as sin, have no brains in particular, yet your health and your will power will win you recognition everywhere.

It is not one bit of use starting muscular and physical development until you have learnt *how* to breathe. Practise this continually until you are master of it. Practise it in the *open air* if you can; best of all in the sunshine, when you not only draw in pure air, but the subtle magnetism direct which is given off by the sun, the centre of magnetism for our wee Universe.

Muscular exercises help us to make and *store* animal magnetism.

The breathing exercises accomplish the same end. The lessons in *concentration* already given help to develop the WILL power, and added to these, you have to consider the question of perfecting the *magnetic gaze.*

The magnetic gaze simply means perfect control of the nerves governing the eyesight, which must be strengthened to that "piercing" degree which can hold another person's eyes, with or against their will.

Coming now to the subject of physical exercises for the muscular development necessary to the storage of magnetism.

Recollect that you must not only take the muscular exercise, but practise correct breathing at the same time, otherwise your pains are wasted.

Stand erect, as directed above, take the dumb-bells and place your hands to your sides, then begin to inhale a long, deep breath—gently, though; no exertion—and as you inhale, slowly lift your arms above your head, till the dumb-bells clash.

Count five, mentally, holding your breath the while; then slowly return your arms to your side, exhaling the breath as you go.

Repeat this twenty times, but remember *very* little benefit will accrue if you forget the breathing and attend only to the exercise. This breathing and muscular exercise tends to strengthen the lungs and chest; and is, simple as it may appear, very valuable.

Continue this exercise DAILY, *with* the breathing exercise.

Now I will show you how to store magnetism for use.

At the close of each spell of exercise, morning or evening as the case may be, or both, draw the breath in as directed before; then as you breathe, slowly stretch one arm at a time straight before you, clenching the hand (without dumb-bells) until every muscle is tense and rigid; relax each arm separately, then repeat with both arms, making both tense and rigid.

Now make each leg, the trunk and backbone, and the neck equally stiff, holding your breath meanwhile, then as you exhale, let every part of your body RELAX, so that you are *limp.* Let your arms sink to your side, your neck and body give way, LET GO everything, be limp as a rag, and so *rest.*

It is not easy, this relaxing process, you want to *relax* the brain too, for otherwise it continues its hold on the muscles and sinews, and in spite of your efforts they remain strained and tense.

Practise an arm at a time, let the fingers hang loose and helpless, then the wrist, and so on, until the entire organism is at your control, to become tense or relaxed as you please.

But, *when* you *tense* your muscles, make them rigid — INHALE YOUR BREATH. When you relax your muscles, EXHALE YOUR BREATH.

It's no end easy to be limp when, like a pair of unworked bellows, you have no air in your lungs; and it's not at all easy to keep rigid with empty lungs. In the next lesson I give a diagram showing the principal muscles, and the best methods of developing them for our present purpose.

LESSON X

To briefly recapitulate the points of the lessons already given, so as to clearly remember *what* personal magnetism is, and *why* the exercises are necessary, I will sum it up under the following headings:—

1st. Personal or animal magnetism is a subtile essence, the nature of which I have already explained.

2nd. It is possessed to a certain extent by most people, but is so faint and undeveloped, it is of little use to them.

3rd. MAN IS A MAGNET, and his strength or weakness depends upon his *knowledge* of the fact, and the development of his thought and will power in response to that knowledge.

4th. Animal magnetism is developed by acquiring *perfect self-control*, and WILL development, and also is very largely dependent upon perfect health.

5th. It is not hypnotism.

6th. By means of it man (and woman) can *attract* people and business, and it is the true key to success in *any* walk in life!

The diagrams of the muscular system of the human frame given with this lesson, will show pretty clearly the effects of the various exercises given for developing personal magnetism.

The exercise of last lesson, as you will readily see, acted upon all those muscles marked "A" in diagrams 1 and 2, those of the chest, abdomen, arms and back.

The *breathing* exercise taken in conjunction with this develops the lungs and sends new blood coursing through the entire body.

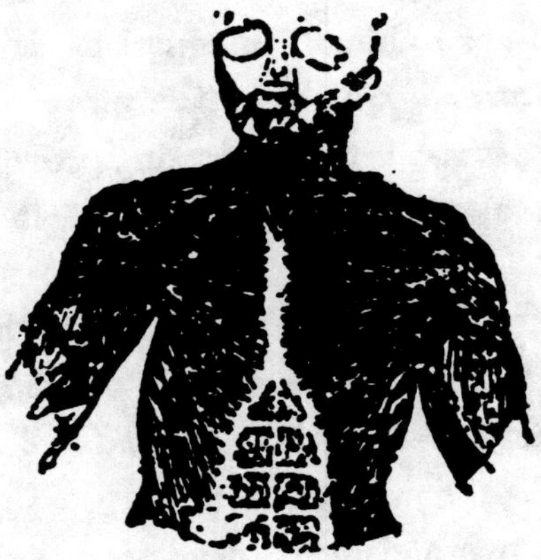

In the directions for *storage* of the magnetism, given in the last lesson, remember the flexing of the body and muscles gives *rest*, the TENSING of the muscles CHARGES THEM WITH MAGNETISM, this magnetism courses through the blood, borne along the crimson tide until it is distributed evenly to every part, *there to be stored and kept for use*, unless

wasted by worry, fear, fidgety ways, lack of self-control, or excess in any form.

The next exercise I want you to take is the American "dry swim." Stand erect, empty your

lungs (exhale), and holding your hands to your sides, gradually sink down into the position of ***sitting on your heels;*** then slowly bring your arms to a horizontal position in front. Then slowly inhale, rising easily and gracefully on tiptoe, throwing the arms back as if swimming, and gradually sinking back on to your heels as before. Repeat this for twenty or thirty times. It is just grand. The blood tingles and courses through the body, and as the blood courses, so the magnetism flows through every vein It is one of the most important exercises, for every muscle is called into play. All the muscles marked "B" in both diagrams, the lungs, and in addition to the lungs, if you follow my directions for correct breathing, given in Lesson IX., every organ of your body also does its proper work.

You cannot be magnetic unless you enjoy perfect *animal* and *mental* health. Correct breathing is the basis of true health, and it helps the nervous system to throw off worry, etc., for *mind* and *lungs* together unite in either perfecting or causing injury to the entire organism.

If the *mind* is depressed by grief, tormented by anxiety, or absorbed in sedentary meditations, all the bodily functions become *weakened*, and personal magnetism, so far from being *stored* to be used to *order*, LEAKS from every pore and is wasted. I can't lay too much stress upon the necessity for proper breathing, or the fact that the exercises are useless, except to develop muscle, not magnetism, unless practised exactly AS I SAY!

The next exercise after the "dry swim" is as follows :—

Stand erect, inhale, then, without bending the knee, bend over until your fingers touch the floor, *exhale* as you rise to an erect position, then slowly inhaling, bend in similar manner to the left side, exhale as you come up, and inhaling again, slowly bend to the right.

This must all be done in a deliberate orderly method, taking about fifteen seconds, or twenty even, for each inhalation and exhalation, then, after tensing the muscles for the storage of magnetism, as taught in the last lesson, rest.

You do not require *any* further physical muscular exercises than these to develop animal magnetism and perfect health, but don't fall into the blunder of thinking you can develop in a *week*. It will take from two to six months of patient, regular exercise, of not *less* than thirty minutes' daily practice, before you arrive at anything like fitness. And in addition to this, you must guard the *mental* portals as well.

Learn to practise concentration, to develop your will, to command your brain and its thought forces. In the next lesson I'll show you the best method of controlling the *nervous* system and *magnetic gaze*.

LESSON. XI

In the previous lessons I have shown you how to develop your lungs and muscles, and so store health and magnetism, and in this lesson we must also consider how to gain complete control over the nerves, both of the body and those connected with sight. The magnetic, or would-be magnetic man or woman who cannot look another full in the face without blinking lacks the most convincing proof of their power.

From the eye proceeds a constant flow of magnetism; it is with the eye "Lion Tamers" hold their captives in thrall; it is through the eye we influence people we come in contact with.

A man instinctively trusts another who can meet his eye with ease, yet many people cannot do this from SHEER NERVOUSNESS.

But before the student can claim a perfect control of all nervous or spasmodic action, he must be able to reserve his power of thus controlling muscular and nervous action under trying circumstances. Among friends, alone, or at one's ease, nerve control is easy enough.

Stand before the looking-glass and practise gazing

into your own eyes until you can do so steadily without flinching for any length of time.

Imagine to yourself a constant stream of magnetism flowing from the eyes.

Practise this upon other people; also force yourself to meet their gaze steadily, and *never forget* that you are the powerful factor, that you are the one to INFLUENCE, not to be influenced.

I could give you several exercises for strengthening the eyesight, but for the magnetic gaze I think you will find the above quite sufficient.

It is not necessary really to go in for more than a few of these exercises.

The basis of all this power is THOUGHT and WILL, and it is not necessary to waste hours in exercises when half an hour twice a day is ample.

Learn to overcome all spasmodic nervous action and trifling habits. Be master of every part of your organisation, through your will power. All the foregoing exercises tend to store up magnetism by giving complete control, so that not only the muscles of the body, but the MIND, the Central Telegraph Office of the body, holds every *nerve* in perfect subjection. Always ready for any emergency, perfect master of yourself and your circumstances, nothing can stand in your path but what your steady flow of magnetism will remove it—*provided your object is a laudable one.*

But one more rule. In the hand of every person there is one spot which is the magnetic centre of the entire being, the little god of flesh, or mount, below the third or "ring finger," called by palmists the Mount of the Sun, or Apollo.

This finger has the most direct nerve connection with the heart, and forms, as I say, a direct magnetic centre, the pad of flesh at the base forming the magnetic pole of same.

So that when people shake hands with the magnetic centres in close contact a strong magnetic current is established between them.

This effect may be intensified if the mounts at the bases of the other fingers are also brought into as close contact with each other as possible, in this way bringing the minor magnetic poles also together.

A handshake can be made to carry out the magnetic influence of eyes and person, by inducing polarisation of the magnetic atoms by contact, which is exactly the course also followed by magnetic healers.

A weak will does not signify a bad man, any more than a strong will signifies a good man.

But a weak willed man is essentially negative, and being so, is more likely to be infirm of purpose in questions of morality.

You have too long been brought up in the belief that you must be the slave of Fate and environment, that the tendencies at birth shape your character, and could not be eradicated.

But the new thought comes to show you that you can both BE and do what you will. Age and sex do not count. The past is over—done with. But the present and the future are your own.

Be positive, send the old negative beliefs flying.

"Let your 'I will have,' wait upon your 'I want.'"

"I will have what I want' will thus carry you through life to a successful goal—to the realisation of all your ambitions.

It has been proved that the particles of an ordinary magnet possess the power of selection, that is to say, they can attract to themselves anything within their own limited sphere of action. The magnet man, on the contrary, has unlimited powers of attraction. Once he knows how to send out his demands, the supply will always be equal to the demand, when the demand is made boldly, without any shadow of doubt or fear.

Man too often *limits himself unnecessarily—he does not demand enough.* Big thoughts carried into action end in big results. Let your sphere of action be as wide as possible; do not go round by the style to escape leaping the big, double blackthorn hedge.

Another great fault is that people are too chary of *giving*, they argue that they have enough for themselves, but not enough to give away. Yet they are drawing upon an *unlimited supply*, the wealth of which is far in advance of the demand—they cannot ask too much, and they cannot give too much.

The most fatal thoughts to success are those of economy, they freeze everything. Nature is *lavish* to the point of extravagance; it is man only who pinches and saves, and *fears* there will not be enough to go round, and so becomes his own utter damnation.

Read Helen Wilman's works on mental science if you want to know more of this law of supply and demand.

LESSON XII

THAT diet plays a large part in the acquirement of Personal Magnetism my readers will readily understand. I have laid down such stringent rul s as to the necessity for *perfect health*, and diet has so much to answer for n the *acquirement* of perfect health, that too much consideration cannot be given to it.

Naturally I do not advocate flesh food in any form, neither do I advise the so-called vegetarian diet.

For perfect health and strength and the "staying" power boasted of by meat eaters nothing can beat a fruitarian diet.

To prove this we need only consider the result of the great International walking race, held at Whitsuntide, in Germany (1902), when the competitors walked from Dresden to Berlin, a distance of 124½ miles.

Thirty-two c mpetitors started from Dresden at 7.30 a.m. on May 18th (1902), in bad weather. Of these men part were fruitarians and vegetarians (including the great Karl Mann, the world's champion walker, of Berlin) part meat eaters.

THE FIRST SIX TO ARRIVE IN BERLIN WERE

FRUITARIANS AND VEGETARIANS, the third man, Martin Rehann, being only twenty years old.

Of course Karl Mann was first, having done the distance in twenty-six hours fifty-eight minutes, and fresh as a daisy at the finish, whilst the meat eaters, well known and tried athletes, arrived utterly exhausted.

George Allen, the English (Leicester) hundred miles walker, is also a vegetarian, and we all know Eustace Miles.

These cases are officially attested, and anybody who likes can verify the statements for themselves.

Karl Mann only takes two meals a day, and he partakes of neither flesh, fowl, alcohol, coffee, tea chocolate etc., and when training, neither eggs, milk, cheese, butter, nor pulse.

We personally, have two meals daily, the first at 12.30 p.m., the second at 6.30, working on the no breakfast plan, which I find splendid for health and a clear brain.

The fruitarian diet is fine, and, to my mind, more satisfying than vegetarianism, to say nothing of what it saves in household work.

However, to the point—it's no use preaching a fruitarian diet if I don't give you practical teaching as to rules, quantities, etc.

I read so much about the beauties of the diet, etc.,

in some fifteen or twenty American magazines, and not one practical hint, that I used to get quite mad, and I firmly believe any number of people would turn from a flesh diet if they only knew how to begin.

The ordinary individual has a tendency to over-eat himself six days out of seven, and to prevent this tendency I advise that a pair of kitchen scales be requisitioned and the proper quantities duly weighed out—indeed this is imperative.

I am allowing the same amount of nutriment for a woman as for a man, but at the same time the fair sex can from the day's allowance knock off a quarter of a pound of dried fruit and half a pound of fresh if necessary.

Personally I think the idea that women eat less than men has arisen because they too often eat *between* meals and men haven't the *chance* as a rule.

Every adult requires from twelve to sixteen ounces of DRY food, *free from water*, daily. To supply this a quarter of a pound of *shelled* nuts and three-quarters of a pound of any dried fruit must be used.

In addition to this from two to three pounds of any *fresh fruit* in season goes to complete the day's allowance.

These quantities should be weighed out and divided in half for the two meals, and will sustain a full grown man in perfect health and vitality. The quantity of ripe fresh fruit may be slightly increased in summer, with a corresponding decrease in the dried fruit.

When beginning this diet it is as well to use a little bread (wholemeal) and plenty of eggs, milk, cream cheese, and cream, until gradually weaned from cereals. Occasionally Quaker Oats and such nut foods as Bromose may be used.

Strawberries, raspberries, cherries, plums, apples. pineapples, grapes, melons, currants, etc., can all be used in summer, and grapes, pears, apples, oranges, bananas etc., in winter.

For the dried fruit raisins, sultanas, prunes, dates, figs and plums, and for a change and stewing purposes we have splendid variety in Californian prunes, apricots, peaches, Bartlett pears, dried apples, bananas and plums.

The nut foods are almonds, walnuts, hazels, cashews, pine kernels, pea nuts (these can be bought *ready shelled*), sapricia, pecan, butter nuts, hickory, brazils (excellent for constipation), Japan pea nuts, chestnuts, and cokernuts.

All these should be got in by large quantities—by FAR the cheapest way—and the diet will be found to pan out at from sixpence, one shilling to two shillings per head daily, according to the *quality* of fruit bought—surely not only a healthier, purer method of living, but infinitely more economical to those who consider such matters!

To cook *dried* fruit, wash it thoroughly in clean water, place it in a dish with enough water to cover it, and soak ten or fifteen hours; then, leaving it in the water it has been soaked in, put it on the stove and let it simmer gently until cooked. When nearly done add sufficient sugar for individual taste. The fruit cooked in this manner very nearly resembles fresh fruit, with the full flavour and taste

English women don't know how to cook dried fruit, and it enters comparatively little into their menus. The above is an American recipe and may be adopted for all the dried fruits, though the dried bananas may be eaten raw or *steamed* in an ordinary potato steamer and eaten with fresh or whipped cream.

Some people advise *regularity* of meals. I advise only two daily, but it is *best* to eat when you are hungry. Al the same you WILL be hungry if you follow the "no breakfast' plan, and able to relish your natural food with a natural appetite

Alcohol kills magnetism.

You will find your magnetic and vital power doubled—nay trebled—by the simple pure food. You will enjoy health such as you never had before, double working capacity, and be able to look God's creatures in the face without a blush.

LESSON XIII

I HAVE shown how Personal Magnetism is largely a matter of health, and the correct storage and increase of the magnetism or electricity contained in our bodies, and the atmosphere upon which we draw to a certain extent for magnetic supplies, although it must be understood we already possess the force in ourselves.

So far the use of animal magnetism for personal advancement has been the object of the lessons given, but there is another side to the question, and animal magnetism for *healing* purposes occupies, in my opinion, a much more important position.

Magnetic healing forms a wonderful means of alleviating pain, and the cures effected by a skilful healer are too numerous to mention.

All nervous diseases, and a good many others, will yield to the treatment, which, needless to say, can only be given by one in perfect health, with a perfect flow of magnetism, and the knowledge of how to treat different diseases.

This requires a certain amount of study on the part of the student, who should have a working knowledge of anatomy, and a good handbook

(Furneaux's is splendid) of physiology is very necessary

Some people say, I know, that I am something of a crank on scientific matters, but I know that until science is linked with metaphysics, the more rational teachings of New Thought will be neglected by the masses.

I advise you to thoroughly study the nervous and muscular system, to gain a good working acquaintance with the various organs of the body and their functions, and a knowledge of the symptoms of some of the diseases the flesh of man is heir to.

In previous lessons you have mastered the art of generating magnetism in the body, and if you have followed the teachings and exercises I have given, you will have a store of magnetism to "give off" for the benefit of others.

If you want to induce a flow of magnetism fo healing purposes, place your hands together in a cone shape and breathe gently into them until they are moist, then rub them briskly together. Repeat this three times when you will have sufficient "flow" for healing purposes.

Begin with the treatment of simple ailments, such as neuralgia, toothache, headache, and so forth and it is for these I will first give you instruction as to treatment.

Always talk to your patient brightly, and try to instil confidence in his mind with regard to your methods.

Stand behind him, and having first generated a flow of magnetism as directed, place your right hand at the base of his stomach and the left at the back of the head, and *will* hard that the magnetism shall flow through the body.

Then lift your hands above his head, and without touching him, make sweeping passes in a downward direction, from head to foot, shaking the hands to "throw off" as you finish each pass.

Open your hands so that the fingers are slightly apart and curved inwards when making the passes.

Then let the patient sit in an easy chair, the head must not rest against the back, or you can't reach him, stand behind him, and treat him with what we call "contact" passes.

The whole time you are manipulating the patient you must steadily WILL that the flow of magnetism from your fingers shall carry away the pain, and leave him free.

First remember that your two hands are, for the time being, converted into delicate instruments, that in fact you carry an electro-magnetic battery in your fingers.

Of this battery you must make your right hand

the *positive pole*, the left hand the *negative pole*. Do not forget this in your treatments, for it is most important.

Now, first place your right hand to the patient's forehead (taking care to press the centre of your palm between the eyes) and the *left* hand at the back of the head; now will earnestly that the magnetic current shall pass through *his entire body*. You force this current through the brain from your *positive* hand, which generates the magnetism, to your *negative* hand, which, being placed at the base of the brain, carries the current right down the spinal column and through the medium of the cerebro-spinal nerves to all the principal organs of the body.

Having done this you now place your hands firmly on the forehead, and stroke from between the eyes, back over the ears to the back of the neck, when the hands are removed and smartly shaken each time as if something sticky was adhering to the fingers.

This is called the "throw off," and carries away the magnetism charged with the pain, thus guarding against the danger of forcing the pain from one part of the body to another.

Continue the treatment until the magnetism is gone, willing steadily the whole time that the pain shall vanish. Remember that the animal magnetism is a FORCE, it is not an effort of the imagination of a few occult cranks. It is a force acknowledged by scientists—French, German, American, and English—men whose names stand high in the world of science and of learning.

Moreover, it is not a mere *theory* on their part, for the flow of magnetism from the human body has been successfully *photographed*, the camera *revealing* that which the eye of man could not see.

Experiment has shown that this force can cure diseases which will not yield to drugs or even ordinary mental treatment.

I have given simple instructions for using the magnetic emanations proceeding from the body for the cure of headache, and now I will show how to cure other diseases of the nervous system.

Let it be understood clearly, however, that magnetic healing will not "set" broken bones any more than Mental or Christian Science will do so. If the Christian and Mental Scientists would take a more rational standpoint and admit certain limitations, they would, at any rate in England, make greater headway. A man who is suffering from a compound fracture of thigh, for instance, won't find it mended by the simple assertion that it isn't broken. So with magnetic healing; but, mark you, *once it has been set by the surgeon, magnetic treatment will cause it to heal up twice as quickly*, for the flow of magnetism induces a flow of newly vitalised blood to the injured part; and those of my readers who desire to take up this business as a means of livelihood should remember this, and recognise the value of the medical man as well as the mistakes he makes.

The solar plexus is the nervous centre of the body which has the most direct connection with the emotions. *Plexus* means a network of nerves and blood vessels, and the *solar plexus* is situated in the abdomen just behind the stomach (not the intestines, be it understood), and is sometimes called the *abdominal brain.* The magnetic healer must not fail to recognise the value of this group of nerves, for a steady magnetic flow induced for ten minutes or so at this part of the body will do much to correct the trouble, no matter what it may be, from which the patient is suffering. Place the right hand over the stomach in front, and the left hand at the corresponding spot behind, and send a steady flow of magnetism right through from one to the other.

It is as well to remember, too, that water or milk can be magnetised, and when given the patient to drink, or to bathe the affected part with, great relief, or even cure, can be brought about.

I cured a bad case of erysipelas by sending the

patient magnetised milk, which she both drank and used to bathe the face.

To do this, pour the milk or water into a scrupulously clean vessel, induce the magnetic flow as already directed, and make passes with both hands over the vessel. Then place the right hand over the mouth of the cup or jug, stiffen the arm, and make the hand vibrate from the muscles of the upper arm (this needs practice), sending a steady flow of magnetism into the liquid.

You can always get into better "touch" with your patient by making him drink some magnetised liquid before treating him. In certain diseases the water may be hot.

When treating for troubles which arise directly from the nerves, place your hands on the seat of the pain and make the currents pass right through from one side to the other. For such things as neuralgia, toothache, earache, etc., make the hands as hot as possible first.

It is usual to give the patient a *general* treatment first of all before attempting to treat locally, and to do this you must proceed as follows:—

Prepare the magnetic flow, and then, having your patient simply garbed in his birthday suit, or a light, loose wrapper, place your right hand at the base of the brain, and pass the left slowly down the spine touching it very gently with the fingers. but sending all your magnetism into the spinal column and directing all your will power to this end.

The patient should take long, deep breaths during the process, breathing from the abdomen.

Now remove your hands and make passes from head to foot—these need not be "contact" passes (that is to say, you do not touch the patient); then treat the solar plexus as already described, and also the chest and lungs in the same manner.

Next, to secure free action of the bowels, place your left hand over the solar plexus in front, and your right at the base of the brain; send strong currents through the body, and *will* that the bowels shall act freely.

Follow this up by a treatment of from five to ten minutes of the *liver*, place the right hand over this organ, and then *vibrate* as I have told you for the magnetised water. Only practice can help you with this; you must *go on* trying until you can do it properly; but it is the most powerful movement you can use.

This profession of Magnetic Healer is one in which money can be made by those who seek a means of livelihood, and can also be used as a means of alleviating much pain and suffering which drugs cannot move.

I agree with the necessity for *surgeons*, but the physician would make more cures if he went in for rational health treatments instead of drugging his patients.

Those of my readers who seek the professional side of magnetism as a healing agent must practise continually, and "treat" everybody they can get hold of.

FURTHER LESSONS ON PERSONAL MAGNETISM

IN the preceding pages I have shown you how to cultivate Personal Magnetism and how, to a certain extent only, to use it

If you have followed the rules carefully, you will at least have learnt a little how to concentrate your mind, and, beyond all else, to have faith in yourself and in your own Power.

This is the groundwork, exactly as the A B C forms the groundwork of languages, but believe me, it is very little more; the true power of magnetism lies in the knowledge of how to apply it, and this I do not suppose one out of a thousand of my students can do on the strength of the previous chapters alone. You have studied the mechanism; you have learnt to believe in the power of one mind upon another: you have practised your scales and five-finger exercises, and now you are ready to proceed to a "*piece*," to play a tune, in fact!

All true magnetic attraction consists of an interchange of magnetism between two centres.

When all is given out and none coming in, the result is utter depletion, so far as the operator goes, and flatness—a grey-drab effect upon the receiver, and is, moreover, absolutely a matter of impossibility to consciously create any effect upon the mind of another person without following certain cut-and-dried rules which are imperative, if any definite measure of success is to be achieved.

Of course you can make another person like you, or you can carry out small schemes, but you are only using the ordinary power of mental attraction, and not true magnetic attraction.

This can only be accomplished when it is accompanied by :—

1. Intensity of purpose.

2. The power of projecting mind images.

3. A knowledge (working) of the true laws of polarity ; and

4. A correct understanding of what I choose to call the magnetic instruments.

So that at once it becomes apparent Personal Magnetism won't be really of much avail for playing monkey-tricks, such as the American guinea courses extol, nor can it be used excepting by a perfectly organized brain, which organization includes self-control.

To attract, you must be indifferent, yet intense of purpose and will.

You must be *patient*, all time is at your command ;

there is no need for haste, but you must understand that, once embarked upon the purpose, whatever it may be, to let go means a weakening of the will force; it is as if the head boy of the class were dismissed to the bottom seat and decked out with the foolscap. Remember that human volition can carry all things before it, but it must be accompanied by faith and persistence.

Also it is no use just *thinking* a thing, it is necessary to ACT; you must translate your thoughts into deeds.

Never waste your efforts on things that do not matter; never fritter your forces away.

To commence with number 4 condition. Under the old law that the first shall be last, and the last first, the correct magnetic instruments are:—

1st. The MIND.

2nd. The WILL power controlling the mental action.

3rd. The EYE.

4th. *The power of touch*, or contact.

5th. *The human voice.*

This last item is never considered in the usual lessons upon this subject, yet it is as powerful in its own sphere of action as the mental side of the question.

The voice can carry magnetism, can stir up hatred or love, can influence the soul with passions or create coldness, it is the most readily used instrument of them all.

But I would have you understand clearly that the conscious brain effort is placed first because it is the chief instrument, and because it is a part of all the rest.

The fine grey matter of the brain records and registers thought images—*thought images, be it said, which can be projected upon the grey matter of another's brain, seized and registered by that brain as its own property*, making it *your* unconscious servant, the doer of *your* bidding, of *your* will, the executor of *your* desires.

And all this without any hypnotic control or without speaking a word.

The will power is the instrument which assists in the projection of these images and which is the leader, the captain of the ship.

In some extreme cases pure desire will accomplish the same end as conscious will effort, but to gain the true effect, the thought must be under the control of the organized will, and for really powerful results to be attained, the determination to succeed must be accompanied by indifference.

For instance, supposing a woman loves a man devotedly, and the man doesn't care a jot if she is alive or dead, that woman is the man's slave, *he* is the centre of attraction, not she; and *he* is the positive pole of which she is a very poor negative.

Now such a woman might try to project a thought to that man's brain, and she could never reach it, she is in the wrong position at the outset, she is not master of herself, but her passions are master of her, and the consequence is she is quite powerless to influence that other person, *however* great her desire.

By indifference you will understand that I mean you must be master of the desire which impels your magnetic action, the desire must not be master of you.

When you are indifferent you are invulnerable.

The man who goes to war praying that he may meet death, returns home with a whole skin.

The man who has plenty of money can go to the race course and bet freely, he will win, it is a matter of indifference to him, whilst the poor beggar whose all depends upon winning will loose everything he has!

Will power is the lever which works the entire mechanism, but will power without the other instruments is no better than mere brute force, it is not magnetism.

The eye, which is the next instrument in power, will always directly stir the magnetic centres, but of course few people ever look one in the eye.

Lessons on Personal Magnetism are careful to instruct students to look at people between the eyes.

Believe me, magnetism only passes when you look *right into* the pupil of the eye — a thing which possibly only occurs between lovers, and which with contact, is more than partly responsible for the thrills which they experience.

The majority of people meet your eye without looking into it. When seeking to influence anybody, look directly into their eyes. Not many people can stand it, and like all magnetic usages it must not ever be abused.

So far as contact is concerned, most of my students and others also know the value of this, and I need not enlarge upon the subject.

Regarding the human voice, it can be directly charged with magnetism, and the sound waves created by it can transmit the message to be sent quite independent of any word effects.

For instance, a woman might be talking a lot of drivel about a summer sale, and yet she may send some strong magnetic force, some powerful magnetic emotion upon the meaningless sound waves.

Of course, to have the strongest effect the words and the emotion should tally, but whereas the mental images projected by the will power may carry any impression from good health to death, from hate to love, and so on, even to certain definite and concerted actions, the voice can carry *emotion only*, but that magnetic emotion properly directed can raise such a storm, such an absolute tornado of corresponding emotion, either in one person or ten thousand people, as to make the uninitiated gasp.

So to recapitulate the use of my five magnetic instruments, the mind is used for creating mind pictures; the will power is used for projecting those mental pictures upon the grey matter of another person's brain; the eye is used for creating magnetic disturbances or explosions in the aura of that other person; the use of contact is for very much the same purpose, whilst the use of the voice is for the conveyance of any particular emotion.

Now we come to number 3: the knowledge of the true working laws of polarity.

As you know from my preceding pages, polarity stands for the positive and negative condition of the magnetic current. We all know that. It is necessary when teaching a pupil music to make him play scales and exercises to render the muscles of the hand lissom, and to give him perfect control over them. Very good.

In my previous work I have emphasized the necessity for becoming positive — the imperative necessity, maybe for *positive* mind action.

Let me tell you now that anybody who uses the positive polarity only soon becomes depleted.

The law is that of the human heart, where the blood beats in and out, of the tides of the ocean, which come and go, of the seasons of the year, of night and of day.

You cannot give all out and take in nothing.

And the great law of polarity is *this:* first *negative* conditions, the taking in; then *positive*, the giving out.

RECEPTIVITY FIRST, THEN IMPRESSION.

This is quite reasonable if you consider the ordinary laws of nature, we do not sow the seed and *then* plough the land, but we plough the land first of all and sow the seed afterwards.

Now I want you to understand the word *receptivity* as synonymous for a process of "*drawing from*," or an inhalation of force, if you can understand that better.

For *impression*, I want you to understand a "giving out," and of the same force that you draw from.

I want to make you understand this clearly, because the whole *use* of magnetism depends on this law, which is seldom or never properly understood.

The main object preached by all teachers of magnetism is *impress, impress, impress!*

You may take it from me that by giving out only impression results in a dull grey or drab effect, there is no play of colour, no real display of power, no definite result.

And all grey or drab magnetism is like any other drab effect, wanting in life, lacking that pulsating sense of colour which arrests the eye and warms the whole being of you.

Of course the next question you will ask is *how* am I to receive, *how* impress? *When* am I to use the one action and when the other? Well, I am coming to that later on. Sufficient for the time being if you will realize the teachings of concentration. The universe is flooded with the power of Universal Attraction.

What *is* Universal Attraction? Some call it one thing, others another.

The Rosicrucians speak of it as great white invisible fire—it is called the universal fluid, the astral light, the odic force, the living, pulsating ether of the ancients. It is enough to understand that this force, call it what you will, floods the universe.

It is in you, it is in me, it is in the space that divides us, no matter if that space is a yard, or if we are separated by half the earth.

This, I think, you all understand; the point I want to emphasize is that this force collects at certain living centres in the body—the solar plexus for one, which is situated at the waist centres of the body.

Some people have it in enormous quantities, others are lacking in it. It is the medium, as I have already explained, which carries our mental messages from one to the other.

By my will power, my breath or my voice, or my touch or my merest glance, I can send my force magnetic from me.

And by those same means I can draw your force away from you, draw it to me.

If I only draw from you, you will become asinine, like an animal, passive sleepy. If I only *send* my force to you, I become limp, weary, inert, lifeless.

But *supposing* that I first draw your force from you to me, and at a given moment *then* proceed to impress my force upon you, alternating the process according to circumstances and conditions, the result will be that you feel alert, charged with new life, strangely excited possibly, thrilled as it were with some curious unknown emotion.

You are receptive, my servant, you accept my thoughts, and you do not know they are my thoughts, you become as one with me, you are for the time being my servant.

And I am quietly charging you with my magnetism, guided by my will, yet without suffering the depletion that would assail me if I had *only* forced my will upon yo

For exercise you may commence this practise with breathing exercises only—and alone!

Stand erect, in a proper physical culture attitude, waist in, chest well breasted upwards.

Now imagine a person, or be content to draw in merely from the universal supply.

Commence by *inhaling* slowly; as you do so, *will* that you draw in the magnetic force from without. You can draw it in with your hands if you like, taking it as if it were something sticky, something that needed a certain amount of *muscle* to bring to you. In other words, a mere light gesture doesn't convey the correct sensation to your brain centres.

Then breathe outwards, still slowly, and as you do it will your own magnetic force outwards and away from you to that other imaginary centre. This for practise only.

You can do the same thing (without the gesture) when you are talking to people. It will not have much effect upon them, because of course it is magnetic breathing only, unaided by the brain, or imaginative side of yourself.

I think you understand this now, and we can leave it *pro tem.* But you can and must practise it regularly.

* * * * *

Now there are two distinct methods of treating

people magnetically. One is what we will call distant treatment, for want of a better name; the other is that treatment used when you are face to face with a person or persons. Curiously enough, the former is infinitely more powerful than the latter, and I will deal with it first of all, although the *modus operandi* in both cases is similar, somewhat, at any rate.

It is not enough to sit down and will that a person shall do so and so, or to even follow up the will conditions with magnetic breathing. To begin with, you must have an absolutely clear conception of what you mean to impress. *That impression must be of the nature of an emotion, and an emotion that is universal. This is the very basic soul essence of your message, it must fail otherwise.*

You can add to that emotion whatever you need to convey, but the emotion is the ground upon which you build your castle, the paper upon which you paint your picture

Before you can send any impression of this emotion, you have to materialize it in yourself.

It is not enough to just think of it in an abstract manner, you will accomplish nothing.

You must absolutely become the emotion, flood your very being with it, shut out every other sensation.

Thus and THUS ONLY can you ever hope to

arouse in that other person the sensation you desire.

Sit down quietly by yourself, and by the aid of your imagination grow into the semblance of your emotion. Any emotion must be universal and freed from all restrictions.

Something which is governed neither by rare creed nor language. Something which the savage and civilized alike feel and understand. Love, hatred, greed, generosity, fear, courage, health, sickness, passion, power, religion—these are all universal emotions, and with one of these, according to your desires, you must be so *saturated* that you are for the time being an embodiment of it, and of it alone.

You are master of this emotion, you have put it on like an overcoat, you can take it off as easily. You are really indifferent.

The next condition still further calls upon our imagination, that wondrous weaver of pictures, of phantasy and fact.

The next step is to see the person you would influence.

This is not difficult to some, to others its acquirement is tedious, but if you have practised concentration you should be able to do it well enough.

You must see them mentally as clearly as if face to face.

Every feature, colour, eyes—all must stand out clearly in your mental vision—Good!

Now, feeling charged with your emotion, with the mental vision clearly before you, call him (or her) by name.

As your voice goes out draw to yourself strongly the magnetic force from that person, as you have been taught, only remember that whereas in practise you draw the force in whilst you are inhaling, here you have to draw it in whilst your voice is ringing outwards, and you may repeat two or three times, just as if you were calling him, and waiting for him to hear you.

Good again!

Now you have gone through three separate phases.

1st. You have created an emotion.

2nd. You have created a mental image.

3rd. You have charged yourself with the magnetism of the person you are acting upon, and by doing this you have created a condition of receptivity in him.

Could you be present with him in the flesh, you would find him restless, a little excited, with his thoughts crowded upon *you*.

It is a very curious thing that the moment you build up a mental image of any person, that person immediately receives a mental image of you.

Now you are ready to send your desire to the person, but do not forget that the desire must agree with the universal emotion, the message *must* correspond. As you transmit your message—aloud—send your magnetic force towards the person with all your will power.

So far as the message goes you must understand that certain cut and dried laws govern this also.

It should be as simple as possible.

It should be capable of translation into a mental picture.

It must be repeated steadily for any length of time necessary.

It depends a great deal upon what the message may be.

You will see from this that telepathy acts as a means of conveying magnetism. But at the same time this method of treatment is really *quite apart* from telepathy as usually understood, excepting so far as the thought images are concerned.

The time required for treatment depends upon your natural ability.

In giving your message never say "*I want*"; that is quite wrong.

Say always "*You want*," for it is the very essence of magnetism that this law shall be observed. *You must throw your thought across the screen of the other person's brain in such form that the thoughts seem their own.*

Perhaps I ought not to speak so freely on these matters, but I know very well there are so few people who can fulfil the conditions or who will persevere, that I do not think there is very much harm done.

Supposing you know somebody who is very unhappy, hopeless, and alone. Satura.e yourself with the emotion of Hope, until you feel buoyant with life and joy.

Call up the image of the person you want to influence, then with the magnetic breathing, call them by name.

Then send your message of magnetic hope: say, "*You want to be cheerful, you want to feel happy; you have your heart full of hope you can sing, you can feel the joy of future success surge through your being*" This will have an altogether different effect to the same treatment delivered by the ordinary means of mental treatment or magnetism

Of course I only take this as an instance. It is by no means the only kind of use to which magnetism may be put. You may want somebody to care for you, or not to care for some other person. You may want somebody to do you a favour, you may be seeking a situation, there are a thousand uses to which it may be put, but the method is always the same, and in the same order.

Coming to personal contact, of course, although in the main conditions are the same, details differ.

And it must be emphasized also that this method is applicable alike to individuals and to audiences.

Actors and actresses can use it, lecturers and preachers, vocalists and reciters, barristers, in fact *anybody* dealing with the general public.

Before you come into touch with either the person or the audience, get a clear idea of your plan of campaign.

What is it you are going to do?

What are your plans?

I will give an instance which really happened to a pupil of mine. He is a business man, and a very big man at that, never mind what sort of business, for that would be telling. Anyway, he had to deal with four men in his own line of business, who had been for years bitterly opposed to certain plans he wanted to carry out, and in no way could he influence them. So he came to me, and I taught him what I have just taught you. To begin with, I made him treat them first from the distance, each man separately. For his emotional saturation I made him take *Power*. Then to each man he gave his ideal, in the form of a mental picture. Next he went to see them, individually. Before entering each man's office he charged himself with magnetism *from* the man in question. Then, quietly talking to him all the time throwing this vivid mental picture upon his brain.

One man capitulated of his own accord without my pupil even putting the question to him at all, and at a public meeting held a few days later the other three men climbed down gracefully, and through the proper use of magnetism gained a victory he had sought for years in vain.

The great difficulty most people will experience in using my method of magnetic treatment, is what I call the emotional saturation.

To a great actress, a Violet Vanburgh, an Ethel Irving, the emotional saturation is a part of their magic, it is easy, to the average English man or woman who has been brought up to stifle emotion, to mask their real feelings until they are sometimes apparently *without* feeling, this assumption of an emotion is difficult.

It is not any use doing it in milk and water fashion.

If you assume the emotion of, say religion you must bring to yourself that intense sensation of awed reverence, as if in the actual presence of the Deity; if you assume the emotion of love, your whole being must pulsate with the tender passion, you become love personified. the *sort* of love is a state of being which must also be considered.

There is a wide difference between the love of a mother for her child, and the love of a strong man for the woman of his heart, or the love of a profligate for some woman who has claimed his butterfly passion. All these shades of difference must be vigorously observed, you must be an *artist;* you do not merely *assume* an emotion, you ARE that emotion for the time, every nerve and fibre of your body responds to the call your imagination makes upon it, and yet you reserve to yourself the right to become instantly calm, normal, unswept by any form of brain storm.

I am not saying it will not take it out of you a little, but as a matter of fact what you lose is infinitesimal if you follow the laws governing magnetic breathing, and properly charge yourself with odic force before you go any further in your efforts, and the emotional storm cannot touch you.

This is one of the reasons why I am so very decided in my teachings as to the due observance of magnetic breathing and the proper use of magnetic polarity.

It stands to reason that if you do not know how to create receptivity, or when to impress, you must be sadly handicapped in the use of this marvellous force, in fact leave out any one item, or transpose them even, and the result will be failure.

Patience, before all things, and faith, the certitude of obtaining results, are essential factors of success, and again the old Biblical saying that with faith you can remove mountains.

However to return to the correct method of dealing with people when using magnetism for what I will call "contact work"—*i.e.*, a personal interview—it must be always remembered that whatever subjects of conversation may arise all the time you are charged with your emotional magnetism until the very air becomes electric (or magnetic) as it were with your purpose.

Learn to talk platitudes whilst you are feeling a great emotion, and learn to *talk* also whilst your brain formulates the words (without speech) which carry your secret will message.

This is by no means an easy task, unless you appear pre-absorbed, which is a wrong attitude and not flattering to the person you have to deal with.

I knew a man once who lost a large fortune through yawning at the wrong moment; and any apparent inattention on your part may do more harm than you imagine.

Learn to smile and look interested, to talk lightly about current topics, all the while your body is seething in a magnetic storm, and your brain hammers out its silent message with the ceaseless insistence which characterizes most forms of suggestion, and, speaking of suggestion, it is always a helpful addition to the use of personal magnetism. The way a word is put will often make all the difference to any result desired.

To say to some people, "*I want you to do so and so,*" is to court refusal. To delicately suggest that it is their own special desire to do this particular thing, will generally result in their believing it *is* their desire.

The whole use of magnetism in its more subtle and useful branches is that of transplanting your own desires to the brain of another in such form that they recognize them only as their own offspring. Constant practice will soon render this easy of accomplishment.

Do not make the common error of over-doing it and growing weary. Personal magnetism is for use, like a pick-me-up, *when needed.* It can be overdone, and the effect lost. After warmth, cold; after night, day; after a magnetic storm of emotion, *rest.*

A pupil of mine, a very dear lady (she is dead now) had a beast of a husband who was always straying away from her. I taught her how to bring him back, but I never could convince her that she must give it a rest.

He came back and woo'd her again as an ardent lover after a fifteen years' coldness and practical desertion, but I never could make her alternate her treatment, and after a year's renewed honeymoon he grew tired again, and once more strayed away from her.

Magnetism appeals so much to lovers that I beg them to remember this law: You can make a man or a woman love you, but if you go on digging it into their brain it grows FLAT, parrot-like and useless.

You achieve your object, very good, give it a rest, do not think of magnetism, don't be too everlastingly sugary, let him (or her) go a little, even alternate your treatment with a little judicious coldness or even neglect, *then* when there is trouble brewing, when the object of your affections grows doubtful, hurt even, uncertain of you, then, if you like, renew your treatment.

Anybody who understands this law of magnetic polarity can hold a man or a woman a willing slave for always. Looks, age, talent, none of these things matter.

But, look you, never grizzle—*never*. Fire up if you must, be cold, be warm, be indifferent, but just take life smiling. The one who goes through life with a song and a smile has a constant magnetic flow. Tears and grizzles will break that flow, you are never magnetic when you grieve. You will get out of the world exactly what you put into it, so be understanding, be sympathetic, be sunshine, and be *strong*.

Never mind what the surface "you" may be. Underneath, let the current of indomitable will guide you on to that which you desire. Once you have put your hand to the plough do not turn back—go on, fast if you can, if not go slowly, but *go on*. If you have begun a thing, if you have formulated a desire, regard it as already your own, for it is so indeed if you have the courage to continue.

To recapitulate the order for personal contact:—

1st. Saturate with your magnetic emotion.

2nd. As you enter the person's presence (with *full lungs* please) and speak the usual greeting, strongly charge yourself with magnetism from them, drawing it to you with your will effort, on the sound waves of your voice.

3rd. Formulate your desires into speechless words, with all the force you are able.

4th. As you formulate charge the person with your own magnetism, the return current.

5th. When you come to the point, which may not always be necessary (in actual words, in fact often it is quite unnecessary to formulate your desires into spoken words at all), but assuming that it is so, let the preamble to your request be an indrawing of magnetism, that is to say, as your voice travels outward along the sound waves it creates your will power, is drawing into you the necessary magnetic charge from the person you speak to, and then when you reach the crisis send voice, will, brain image all heavily charged with your own magnetism *outwards* to the person you are dealing with. You will be astonished at the effect, if a strong electric battery were played upon him he could not be more influenced, and it is very seldom indeed that such a charge will fail.

Public speakers, and so forth, can use this power in the same way, of course much depending upon what their subject may be, but it's no earthly use unless pre-charged with the correct magnetic emotion; that is your groundwork, and whatever your outward words or actions may portray, you must not lose sight of that for a moment. It must be felt, it must radiate from you with an intensity that all can feel and understand without speech or action to explain your purpose. As my infant son says when he turns head over heels, or tries to, "that takes a bit of doing"—but whoever can do it is master of a force greater than any other force known to science as yet, master of a power one almost hesitates to use. Let your use of it be for good only, or believe me it will turn and rend you!

O HASHNU HARA.